I REJOICE IN MY CHAINS

Memoirs of Bishops and Priests in Prison

SAINT SHENOUDA PRESS

I REJOICE IN MY CHAINS

Memoirs of Bishops and Priests in Prison

ST SHENOUDA PRESS

SYDNEY, AUSTRALIA

2021

I Rejoice in My Chains:
Memoirs of Bishops and Priests in Prison

ST SHENOUDA PRESS

8419, Putty Rd,

Putty, NSW, 2330

Australia

www.stshenoudapress.com

ISBN 13: 978-0-6485754-0-5

Translated by: Michael Kozman

CONTENTS

INTRODUCTION

History tells of political and social unrest in Egypt around the time of President Anwar Sadat in 1981. President Sadat exiled H.H. Pope Shenouda III to the monastery of St. Bishoy on the 3rd of September 1981. What followed was the imprisonment of several Bishops and laymen without any justifiable cause, in what became a very unsettled time in Egypt. The conditions of their imprisonment were abominable. They were subjected to horrid living conditions and psychological warfare from their guards and interrogators.

This book recounts a translation of extracts from the personal memoirs of people who were with H.H. Pope Shenouda and Bishop Beimen, as well as accounts from Bishop Benyamin, Fr. Boules Basili and Fr. Youssef Asaad.

This book conveys very personal and moving accounts of those who experienced first-hand the persecution during this tumultuous time. The memoirs also recount their faith, power of prayer and experience of God's guiding hand to facilitate their release.

UNDER HOUSE ARREST

POPE SHENOUDA III

By: Bishop Beimen

On the 25th of April 1982, Israel agreed to complete its withdrawal from the Sinai Peninsula and return the land to Egypt. However, the Israeli negotiators threatened to cancel the peace treaty by fabricating a story that there was incomplete normalisation between Egyptian and Israeli people (normalisation was one of the conditions for the peace treaty). The negotiators used the fact that Egyptians were banned from visiting Israel to push their agenda.

Egyptian president Anwar Sadat[1] gambled with his political connections to try to obtain peace with Israel. Commentators have likened this political move to a person carrying his coffin to the enemy and being under their mercy. President Sadat experienced political isolation from neighbouring Arab countries to allow the complete Israeli withdrawal and decided to silence the voices of his adversaries; including the religious rebellion of Islamic groups and some Copts, both laymen and priests. As such Sadat tried to portray 'equality' among both Copts and Muslims and show that sectarian violence existed among both religions. At the same time, our beloved Pope Shenouda III advised the Coptic congregation to avoid visiting the Holy Land of Jerusalem as a political statement demonstrating the need for the peace treaty to proceed and to avoid any conception that the Copts were traitors against the Palestinian position. This strained the relationship between President Sadat and Pope Shenouda,

---

1 Whose full name is Mohamad Anwar Mohamad Mohamad El-Sadaty

and thus President Sadat ordered for the house arrest of His Holiness inside the monastery of St Bishoy in Wady El-Natroun. He also appointed a committee of five bishops to run the affairs of the church in his place.

President Sadat overlooked the fact that the selection of the Pope in the Coptic church occurs independently, guided by the will of God after extensive prayers, and any interference in the Church would have severely negative consequences. President Sadat also issued a warrant for the arrest of; eight bishops including Bishop Beimen, twenty-four priests, twenty-four servants and eighty-five laymen. In fact, President Sadat imprisoned nearly all the bishops who were ordained by Pope Shenouda and also many influential priests and servants. In addition, President Sadat ordered the imprisonment of innocent civilians who were already being persecuted for alleged rebellion and sent them to a facility called the 'prison of trials' inside El-Marag prison. It did not appear to the president that the people he imprisoned were very dear in the eyes of God and the Coptic congregation.

The living circumstances inside El-Marag prison were extremely harsh for the Coptic prisoners, especially those who were sick such as Bishop Beimen, as opposed to non-Coptic people who were imprisoned in drastically better conditions.

In one of the national celebrations taking place on the 6th

of October in 1981, President Sadat refused to wear a bullet-proof vest and requested that his personal guards stand afar to improve his appearance in the presence of the media. Unfortunately for him this had a devastating outcome as it significantly contributed to his assassination. After President Sadat's assassination, all those imprisoned were treated well and eventually released.

I will now attempt to reflect on the events that led to this outcome.

FREEDOM

In the memoirs of Pope Shenouda from his time under house arrest in the monastery of St Bishoy, he spoke with journalist

Mohamed Fawzy and said the following:

> "I naturally like the monastery and the life of calmness and serenity. When I was ordained a monk, I never thought that I would have to go back to the world and take on any worldly duties. All I wanted was to grow in the life of solitude and reach its depths. Monasticism, as I know it, is separation from all to be with the One. The 'One' is God."

> Pope Shenouda wrote, "I remember a poem that I wrote

on my way to the monastery which was a contemplation on the anchorites. This is a level in monasticism where one dwells isolated in the desert wilderness, not knowing where they are, nor the world knowing anything about them. They commit their whole life to God". I wrote:

I was aiming for a life like this, in which a person would live in total isolation and continual connection with God. However, God did not allow this for me. When President Sadat allowed me to go and spend forty consecutive months in the monastery, I took it as a good chance to return to the life of solitude and contemplation, even if it was forced upon me externally, I enjoyed this time thoroughly.

During this period, I published 16 books due to the calmness, solitude and recollection of my thoughts. I always try to leave all my troubles behind. I believe that a person should maintain their inner peace in their heart, not allowing any external circumstance to overcome them. Rather, they should overcome their troubles through faith, serenity and complete surrender to God. The aim is to capitalise on the spiritual benefits that can come from tribulations.

I used to tell people that the source of tribulation is a

hard heart, as the hard heart does not accept tribulations. Therefore, tribulations usually arise from within the heart rather than external circumstances. If, however, the heart widens to accept tribulations then there would be no tribulations at all. I always obtain inner peace internally rather than from external sources, and thus I considered myself to have returned back to the life of solitude of which I originally became a monk. Everyone who saw me only witnessed a smiling face, always accepting distress."

CONFINEMENT IN ST BISHOY'S MONASTERY

Bishop Pasante, who was the secretary for Pope Shenouda from January 1981 until 1986, in his book, The Harvest of Years, recounts that between 5th December 1981 to 5th January 1985, (the period of Pope Shenouda's 'house arrest'), the Pope used to humbly help the workers carry buckets of mud to plant in the garden beds of the monastery. During this time, Bishop Pasante sometimes saw His Holiness sitting in the dust and asked him if he could get him a chair, to which His Holiness always responded saying, "we are dust and are sitting on dust." [2]

During this hard time, His Holiness gave the workers spiritual lessons with simplicity of heart. He said, "God wanted us to serve among people. We thank God. God wants us to serve

---

2 The Harvest of the Years, Part 1, page 48

in the monastery. We thank God again." Some visitors also commented that while he was imprisoned, Pope Shenouda said to them, "A man imprisoned in paradise. Is there anything better than that?!" By his joyful nature, His Holiness was able to strengthen and comfort the souls of all who visited him.

Due to his life of faith, His Holiness received the gifts of peace and joy. His Grace Bishop Pasante reflects on the strength demonstrated by St Anthony written by St Athanasius, "If anyone is troubled and sees St Anthony, they would return filled with peace. If anyone indulges himself in the world and then sees St Anthony, he will become a person who indulges in the heavenly." Bishop Pasante continues, "I have seen so many metropolitans and bishops visit His Holiness being overwhelmed with sorrow and grief, but when they see his simple and joyous attitude, they were made joyous and peace filled their hearts."

While under house arrest, His Holiness invested his time with work that would be beneficial for the entire nation. He wrote letters encouraging the faithful to respectfully welcome the new president Mohammad Hosney Mubarak. He also wrote books that are now considered important spiritual resources such as 'The Life of Repentance and Purity' and 'Life of Faith'. It was also a beneficial time for the monks in the monastery as Pope Shenouda would often give deep spiritual sermons to his fellow monks. His Holiness contributed to the renovations and developments in the monastery, particularly farming, and continued to tend issues pertaining to the Coptic Church worldwide.

THE RELEASE FROM HOUSE ARREST

Mr Victor Salama, vice editor of the newspaper "Watani", described the release of His Holiness saying, "The feast of Nativity is upon us and the nation impatiently waits for the return of His Holiness in order to celebrate the feast of Nativity with all the congregation." Truly, this was a special event. After a long imprisonment, the whole world was waiting for the release of Pope Shenouda from house arrest. When the date of his release was revealed, many national and international news channels rushed to St Bishoy's monastery, eager to obtain an interview from him before leaving the monastery. Journalists from Watani newspaper documented a detailed description of the events that took place during his release.

Pope Shenouda gave an interview in a conference with the media where he was visibly overwhelmed by the media attention and inquiries. Some of his answers were just simple smiles, but other responses were answered in some details.

Some of the questions and answers below:

Q. How did you receive the order for your release?

A. The order was not a surprise to me because it was preceded with many steps and all these steps finally led to the order for my release. Truly, I received the final order of release with joy for the sake of Egypt. Since being released, Egypt became free from all other decrees that were given in September and this was the last decree to be issued. I was also happy for my release for the sake of the Coptic nation because their problem was finally solved, and I think this order was crucial for the unity of our nation.

Q. Does this order mean that you have freedom of speech?

A. Freedom of speech has always been protected and I never lost this freedom. It is the freedom of movement that is now restored.

Q. Do you wish to continue having the monastery as a papal residence or do you wish to relocate the papal residence to Cairo?

A. Where the Pope is, there is his residence. I never gave up the monastic life even before I was imprisoned in the monastery. I always used to spend some of my time during the week in the monastery, and the rest of my time in Cairo and Alexandria.

I think that both residences will continue in Cairo and the monastery, because it is part of my freedom of movement.

a) Are there any arrangements concerning your return to Cairo?

My departure from the monastery will be in complete silence and no one will know when I leave. I do not want to load my children with the heavy burden of waiting for my return or cause any traffic congestion problems.

b) What arrangements are in place with regards to praying the feast of Nativity?

The entry of Coptic Christians will be by special invitation only to avoid overcrowding, which would be nearly impossible for us to manage and no cars will be allowed to park on the premises to avoid congestion in the area.

c) Will you form an office for national unity upon your return?

Regarding an office for national unity, I would rather leave this matter up to the government to maintain national unity more effectively. As I mentioned previously, I hope that the government forms an office for national unity; either through the president of Egypt or the department of internal affairs. It's important that someone from the government controls and oversees it.

d) What is your role in this matter?

All that I will be trying to do is deepen the love and peace between the church and the nation, and between our church and the Muslims. This is the matter that I wish we could address continually. We wish to live in love with each other, as members of the one body of the Egyptian nation. I am willing to take all the available measures to reach my goal, not by myself but with my beloved bishops and priests, as we all have the same willingness to live in Egypt in peace, calmness and serenity.

e) What is the next plan for your Holiness in the coming days?

I have no action plan. All our plans as religious men are directed towards spreading love among all people. This is our message for which we work, to create good relationships among each other and the Lord.

If any misunderstandings have occurred throughout the past, it was unintentional. The main condition of our message is love; whoever moves away from love becomes an obstacle as we want to live in love with everybody.

I am personally willing to carry out any suggestions that would positively deepen the love in Egypt. It is for the greater good of the nation to avoid divisions. We all know that the normal status in Egypt is love rather than divisions. Contentions are not a norm, and people cannot live in an atmosphere of contention. There must be a calm and peaceful atmosphere among us to be able to love everybody.

EVENTS THAT LED TO HIS
HOLINESS' HOUSE ARREST

Sectarian conflict leading to the issuing of the warrants for imprisonment of Pope Shenouda the Third:

1. The amendment of the second point of the constitution in 1971 about the Islamic religion as the national religion, by adding the sentence "The Islamic constitution (Shariah) is a source of national law." This sentence was later changed in 1979 to read, "The Islamic constitution is the major source of national law." A committee of men from El-Azhar set laws originating from the Islamic constitution, such as whipping for drinking alcohol or drunkenness and the cutting off a hand for stealing. Prosecution of an alleged crime had to be confirmed by two Muslim witnesses of legal age. Non-Muslims could not be witnesses.

2. The attack on the Orthodox resurgence society in Damanhour on 8th September 1972, where explosives were thrown inside the building as a response to the printing of a hundred copies of an alleged report written by Pope Shenouda attacking Islam.

3. The burning of the church of the Orthodox Holy Bible society in El-Khanka on 6th November 1972. It was burnt down again the following Sunday on 12th November. Several priests, accompanied by four hundred of the laity, prayed in the remains of the church. On the same night, some extremists burned and vandalised a few houses nearby.

4. The tragedy of the church in El-Ayat in Giza in 1973. After the church had received a presidential approval to be built, some Islamic extremists prevented and attacked the builders. The digging of the foundation for the building ceased.

5. In June 1975 St Mary church in El-Bitakh, around the district of Souhag, was tragically attacked and vandalised. Some Copts were seriously injured in this attack.

6. The tragedy of the church in El-Mahamda near the district of Souhag, where both Fr Dawood and Rev Fr Kyrillos were attacked and became unconscious. Similar events also occurred in the church of Archangel Michael in El-Awaysa, district of Samalout.

7. Apostate law: the sheikhs of el-Azhar university brought forth the apostate law in January 1977, which stated that whoever renounced the Islamic religion would be killed. This rule applied to Muslims who renounced the Islamic faith and converted to Christianity or if a Christian who initially renounced Christianity reverted back to Islam. The sheikhs tried to push for a bill to pass this law in the People's Assembly. It is important to mention that the apostate law is against the Islamic religion and freedom of one's universal human rights amongst other things. Concerning this issue the Holy Synod ordered a strict fasting with abstinence of three days from Monday the 5th of September 1977 until Friday the 9th of September 1977, and fasting without abstinence on Saturday and Sunday. At the request of the Holy Synod; Bishop Antonious, Bishop Samuel, Bishop Youannes and Bishop Bishoy went to the presidential palace and handed a letter stating the church's objection to the attempt to implement Islamic Law. Vice President Mamdouh Salem, in return, visited Pope Shenouda and advised him that the apostate law did not convey the general consensus of the government.

8. The incident of St Mary's Church in the district of Monakateen in Samalout with the foreclosure of the church to appease the extremists in May 1977.

9. The incident in the city of El-Tawfeekia in Samalout in June

1978, where a religious dispute occurred and a vicious attack was carried out on ten Coptic households. The dispute was the conversion of a Muslim man named Wahib to Christianity. The priest who led him to Christianity, Fr Gobrial Abdel-Motagally, was martyred after advising him not to forsake his Christianity.

10. In March 1978, a decision was made by the department of education to force all university students to study Islam as a compulsory subject. Students who did not successfully complete the course would fail to graduate. Pope Shenouda sent a rebuttal and disagreement to this proposal; however, it was discarded.

11. A 32-year-old priest from the church of St John the Baptist was executed in the district of Doweeka by the hands of extreme Islamic groups on 24th November 1978 and no conviction was made for the murder.

12. On 24th February 1979, the church of St John the Baptist in the district of El-Zawya in Assiut was closed after an attack by extreme Islamic groups.

13. The burning of the church in Kasreyat El-Rehan on 19th March 1979, when the church was completely engulfed in flames. Coincidentally, the water supply from that region was cut off before even the fire started. This church was a great

building made entirely of wood and was at least 15 centuries old. This incident occurred when the American President Jimmy Carter visited Egypt in attempt to attain peace between Egypt and Israel. The government promised to rebuild the church, but this never happened.

14. Bombing of St George's church in Sporting, Alexandria on the eve of the feast of Nativity on 7th January 1980, while another bomb exploded nearby.

15. Persecution of Christian university students to prevent them sitting their final year examinations. One example occurred in the university of Alexandria on 18th March 1980 where ten students were injured and taken to hospital, while other students were imprisoned.

16. In June 1981, the church witnessed one of the most gruesome incidents at the hands of extremist Islamic groups. A dispute arose regarding ownership of a piece of land in El-Zawya El-Hamraa, despite being owned by the church Islamic extremists suddenly claimed ownership of the land. This argument violently escalated on 17th June 1981, when Muslims clashed with Christians for a second time leading to the death of 81 Copts. The government did not intervene for three days. Among the killed included; V. Rev. Father Maximous Gerges who was murdered after being asked to proclaim the Islamic

faith, to which he refused, leading to slashing his throat and receiving the crown of martyrdom.

17. When the supplies of the extremist Muslims dwindled, they resorted to stealing gold and jewellery from Coptic shops, such as what happened in Nagaa Hamady on 26th June 1981. Three Copts and two Muslim people were caught in the cross-fire between police and the Muslims during an attempted robbery and were killed. Also, in Shobra El-Khema on 31st July 1981 some Christians were injured due to extremist violence.

18. On 2nd August 1981, an explosion occurred in the church of St Mary in Mesra (Shobra) during the wedding of Marcel Samuel and Nabil Habib. 59 people were killed; including 14 Muslims.

19. National television hosted a program for Shiekh Mohammad Metwally El-Shaarawy every Friday to explain Quranic verses, but on one occasion he chose to attack Christian doctrine. This led to planting the seeds of conflict between Christians and Muslims, which subsequently impacted national unity. This moved Bishop Gregorious, the church Representative, to send a letter to the minister of marketing and cultural education to protest about the incident and explain the potential dangers.

A STRAINED RELATIONSHIP BETWEEN
POPE SHENOUDA III AND PRESIDENT MOHAMMAD
ANWAR SADAT

The series of events that led to a strained relationship between His Holiness Pope Shenouda III and President Mohammad Anwar Sadat between 1980 and 1981 were as follows:

When the Copts rallied to show their disapproval about the burning of a Coptic Orthodox church, President Sadat viewed the rally as a rebellion against himself despite both Pope Shenouda and the fellow committee members of the Holy Synod requesting his involvement in solving issues that faced the building of churches when he visited the Patriarchate of St Reweis in El-Abbaseya in December 1972. President Sadat said to Pope Shenouda: "I will give you fifty approvals per year," limiting the construction of churches to that number. President Sadat even went inside one of the rooms of the Holy Synod in the episcopate to pray! However, after visiting the Patriarchate a second time on 11th October 1977 he had only given fifty-eight approvals since 1972.

During the second visit of President Sadat to the Patriarchate, he established construction for the new St Mark Hospital to be built on the ground of St Reweis church. Pope Shenouda gave a very pleasant speech after this announcement praising him. President Sadat wanted to influence him by donating fifty thousand pounds for the construction of the hospital, which would come out of the presidential fund. Unfortunately for a long period of time, construction for this new hospital remained just a foundation stone as many obstacles impeded the building of the hospital, such as the accusation that construction would be detrimental to other surrounding hospitals. Finally though, the building was completed and soon after President Sadat received a golden medal for peace on 17th December 1978 from the Methodist Church. He presented this medal to Pope Shenouda, in attempt to appease the authorities and was surprised when he to accompany him on his presidential visit to Jerusalem in 1977.

In July 1981, President Sadat travelled to America to meet with the newly elected president Ronald Regan. At the same time, Coptic councils in America published an article in the Washington Post and the New York Times explaining the tyranny of the Egyptian government against the Copts in Egypt. This led to riots breaking out against President Sadat in the capital city of Washington, with one riot even occurring just outside the white house during his visit to America. Another riot occurred outside the Metropolitan Museum which Sadat visited after they established a new department for Egyptian archaeological findings. Pope Shenouda sent Bishop Samuel (Bishop of general services and overseas churches) to the United States in attempt to appease the Coptic people rallying and to avoid further infuriating President Sadat.

Mr Mohammad Hesein Haikal says in his book 'The Autumn Anger':

"President El-Sadat was in an awkward position, because he had promised the Israelis a peace agreement which included exchanging tourism in both countries. However, the position of the Egyptian community was in great disagreement with the peace agreement. President Sadat claimed that he had a 'revelation' to solve this issue. It had occurred to him that the border entry of Egyptians into Jerusalem had been closed since 1967, before which time there used to be between forty and fifty thousand Egyptians visiting Jerusalem for pilgrimage every year. The 'revelation' of President El-Sadat was to allow the resuming of pilgrimage to Jerusalem to restore a balance of tourism in both countries. President Sadat went ahead to notify Pope Shenouda that, "Since the relationship had been restored between Egypt and Israel, it gives me great pleasure to notify His Holiness that the pathway of pilgrimage has been restored." It was a great surprise though for President Sadat when Pope Shenouda refused this 'revelation'. His response was, "Please tell President Sadat that the problems that set aside Egypt from the rest of the Middle-Eastern world will dissolve one day, and I do not want the Coptic Egyptians to betray the Arab world until things return to their original status between surrounding countries. It is therefore not the right time for the Copts to resume pilgrimage to Jerusalem."

Lieutenant Mohammad El-Nabawy Ismail, minister of internal affairs said during the September events of 1981:

"President Sadat ordered the events of September 1981 to proceed as a retaliation to some movements of opposition, which lead to some voices in Israel to retaliate by refusing to give up Sinai to Egypt according to the peace agreement. The president saw that it was fit to keep the opposition in custody until they were set free on 25th April 1982 as a celebration for reclaiming Sinai."

On 26th March 1980, the Holy Synod decided that they would not accept greetings for the feast of the Resurrection on 7th April 1980 from governmental bodies, nor would they allow these greetings to be aired on national television or newspapers due to the persecution of Christians that was occurring at that time in Egypt. The bishops were asked to pray the feast of the Resurrection liturgy in the monasteries. Continued escalation occurred when President Sadat alleged accusations against Pope Shenouda III, stating that he was putting national peace and unity in jeopardy by encouraging hatred and disarray in the country, and using religion for diplomatic and political purposes.

The President issued a decree in 1981 abolishing the presidential ruling which stated that Pope Shenouda III is the patriarch over the See of St Mark.[3] By revoking Pope Shenouda's signature, he was no longer allowed to be present in Cairo or Alexandria, thus no longer allowed to meet with his congregation. President Sadat formed a committee of five bishops to cover the duties of the Pope. The Committee of Five included:

1. Bishop Maximous of El-Kaliobeya

2. Bishop Samuel of general services and overseas churches

3. Bishop Gregorious of scientific research and Coptic studies and general officer of the high college of Coptic studies

4. Bishop Athanasius of Bani Sweif and El-Bahnasa

5. Bishop Youannes of El-Gharbeya and Secretary of the Holy Synod

On Wednesday 30th September 1981, Talat Younan, a journalist and secretary for Dr Kamal Ramzy Estino who later became a journalist for the famous El-Ahram newspaper, took issue against His Holiness and wrote a 150 page article directed to President Sadat explaining the history of the Church and

---

3 Ruling number 2782 of the year 1971

major disagreements that had occurred in it. Talat Younan also concurred with the President's decision to relieve Pope Shenouda of his papal duties with the aforementioned committee. Talat Younan also accused the Pope of kindling a fire of religious contention. Somewhat interestingly Talat Younan passed away of a heart attack and his obituary was on the second last page of the same newspaper written against the Pope. His family found it extremely difficult to find a church that would pray over his body. Indeed, it is written, "No weapon formed against you shall prosper" (Isaiah 54: 17).

An old lady who was famous for serving the poor and the needy, known as Mother Abdel-Sayed (Mother of the Poor), said about President Sadat, "God will take revenge on this man within 40 days." And indeed, it happened that within 40 days of her statement that President Sadat was assassinated.

After Pope Shenouda complained to the justice office they ruled in his favour against the outcomes of the decisions made against him in September 1981. In April 1983, a decision was made to abolish the committee that President Sadat had formed earlier to replace the Pope. This decision was made in the courtroom under the ruling of Galal El-Din Abdel-Hameed and Abdel-Aziz Amer. Another ruling was made to revoke all the decisions made in September 1981 under the ruling of Mr Yehya El-Boshra, vice president of the government ministers, and

Mohammad Ibrahim Ahmad. The number of Muslim lawyers outnumbered the number of Coptic lawyers. The most famous of these lawyers included; George Alexander, Greek minister of justice, Mr Ahmad Khawaga, Mr Ahmad Nabil El-Helaly and Mr Morris Sadek.

Finally, President Mubarak put forth a presidential decree to re-instate Pope Shenouda as the Pope of Alexandria and Patriarch of the See of St Mark.

THE BISHOPS

Since President Sadat was furious about some of the actions of Pope Shenouda, he captured and imprisoned eight bishops that were ordained during his papacy.[4] All of these eight bishops were captured on Thursday 3rd September 1981, except for Bishop Bishoy and Bishop Tadros. Bishop Bishoy was accompanying H.H. Pope Shenouda in St Bishoy's monastery when the police came to its gate on Saturday 5th September 1981. He turned himself into the police after taking permission from Pope Shenouda and was arrested.

Bishop Tadros was at a conference in Cyprus at the time when he heard that an arrest warrant was out for him, yet he insisted on returning to Egypt. He could have chosen to stay in Cyprus,

---

4 Refer to Appendix for the list of Bishops and Priests who were imprisoned.

or even flee to America as he became an American citizen after serving there for several years. After returning to Egypt, he was captured at the airport. When he was placed in handcuffs, he bent down and kissed them. As the police led Bishop Tadros directly to prison he was saying this verse, "choosing rather to suffer affliction with the people of God than to enjoy the passing pleasures of sin" (Hebrews 11: 25). When the fathers in prison asked him what he felt after being handcuffed, he said, "They felt like golden bracelets."

THE PRIESTS AND LAYMEN

For President Sadat to appear as though he was not only imprisoning religious men, he needed to give the impression that he was capturing both Muslim and Christian extremists alike. If he had only imprisoned Muslims, then having religious contentions would not have been a valid excuse and thus some attempt at 'equality' was needed by imprisoning other Christians such as:

(a) Laymen accused of religious contentions. Their names were mentioned in the police file and numbered about 85 people, of which 24 had been involved with church renovations.

(b) Priests and servants who tried to respond to the attacks of Sheik Mohammad Metwally El-Sharawy against Christianity in his religious program that was aired every Friday on Egyptian national television

It was almost as if the authorities were punishing those who protested against Christian persecution. Saad Zaghlool, an Egyptian revolutionary and statesman, once said, "before you tell someone to stop crying, tell the other person to stop hurting," and this reflects the circumstances of the church at the time of the imprisonments.

Several Christian laymen, about 85 in number, were also imprisoned for fighting with Muslims and imprisoned at Abu-Zaabal, near the prison of El-Marag. They were placed with five people in each cell, given one bucket to use as their toilet and were very poorly treated. Twenty-four of those imprisoned were accused of aiding in the restoration of churches and were kept with the priests imprisoned in El-Marag. Fr Athanasius Boutros Soliman, of the Church of Archangel Michael and St George in Matarya, commented about this, "The police imprisoned every bishop, priest or layman who could potentially affect the general population. President Sadat's decree in 1981 ordered the foreclosure and ceasing of two newspapers that were Coptic based; namely El-Keraza and Watani. This was done so that the Muslim community could accept the foreclosure and ceasing of the printing of their newspaper El-Daawa."

341 DAYS IN PRISON

BISHOP BENYAMIN
OF AL-MONOFEYA

Two days before I was imprisoned, I attended a celebration with my congregation on my anniversary as a bishop. I invited all the state security officers of the area, the mayor of Mooneye Al-Monofeya and other government officials to celebrate with us. At the time there was not a trace that a problem would arise. The following day I had a spiritual retreat in Al-Balyana for the day and returned home late in the evening.

On the 3rd September 1981, I received a phone call from the head of state security at 10 a.m. asking to meet at my residence, and shortly afterwards we arranged a meeting at midday. At around 11:45 a.m. I received information that the head of state security had arrived while I was in my office with some guests until midday. I then walked down to greet the head of state security and he quickly requested that we go upstairs to receive a call from lieutenant Hasan Abu-Basha through the wireless police radio phone. At the time I was completely unaware of what was going on and I thought that making a wireless phone call with the lieutenant was probably only because the phone lines were down. I accepted with an open heart to go back into my office and both the head of state security and myself sat down waiting for about 20 or 30 minutes without receiving a phone call. I asked him if the phone call had been delayed, to which he responded "No, the phone call indeed occurred, and the lieutenant wants you to come with me to Cairo for questioning."

During this meeting one of the people present in my office was the secretary of the committee, a lawyer named Shafeek Zaki. Mr. Shafeek asked him, "Why do we have to meet in Cairo? Do you have an official warrant to summon His Eminence?" The officer replied, "Mr. Shafeek, please do not intervene in this matter. Do not say another word." Then I immediately felt that something was wrong. I said to the officer, "It seems that there is something going on that we don't quite understand yet, however, regardless of whatever they do to us we will be considered worthy of suffering disgrace for His name. If we're going to Cairo, please allow me to get my bag and have the driver bring the car to take us there". The officer responded saying, "My apologies, but I cannot let you leave this room." I tried to reason with him, "Why? Am I under arrest?", and he responded, "I cannot disclose such information." At this point, all I could say to him was, "I am at your disposal. Do what you need to do."

I called one of the consecrated deacons to grab my bag from another room and went with the officer to his car. I sat next to him in the car with two accompanying police officers in front of us. We were then taken to the El-Marg Prison. On the way to the prison, I took out my Agpia (Prayer Book), and began to pray the psalms quietly and peacefully. I could see ahead of us an ambulance and a police car with armed police officers behind us. I thought to myself, "This is what the Lord Christ said when

He was arrested. 'Have you come out, as against a robber, with swords and clubs to take Me?' (Matt 26: 55)"

When we arrived at El-Marg Prison I was escorted to the warden's office, where the warden and some governmental agents were seated around him. The warden asked me to remove all my belongings and place them on the desk, except for the clothes on my back. When I told him that I was wearing my belt of monasticism, he said, "Please go to the room next door and take it off." He was very polite and respectful. After all my belongings were confiscated, including my hand cross and cross around my neck, I was escorted to prison cell 11. This prison cell was known as "the Prison of Trials" as it was the toughest place in the prison. I ended up spending about 40 days locked up inside there.

This prison cell was quite dark, much like a sepulchre. The officer who was escorting me, named Ali, was given an order to give me 'special food', of which I thought would be poisonous in attempt to kill me. The officer then locked the door of my cell and left to bring some food. I looked around, only to see that the things inside the cell were at a bare minimum, except for a mattress, pillow, and an open toilet in a small 1.75 m2 dark cell. I knelt and kissed the floor of the cell, then stood up to pray in preparation to die from food poisoning. After I finished praying, I sat down on the mattress and later the cell door unlocked.

I thought, 'the food is here, this must be the end!'. Yet to my surprise, I saw Fr. Basilious and Fr. Sidrak, both priests from El-Minya being escorted into my cell. When one of the priests saw me, he exclaimed, "What?! They even arrested a Metropolitan?!" The officer escorting him said, "This man is from El-Minya, and that man is from Al-Monofeya. This must be a gang that we're rounding up!" We warmly embraced each other and sat down talking for a while, catching up on what was happening outside. Shortly after another man named Tharwat, a Mathematics teacher at a high school in Assiut, was also imprisoned into our cell.

Later that night one of the prisoners in another cell, a journalist named Samir Tadrous, stood at the door of his small cell announcing to everyone to come to their cell door and take turns in recording their name, where they're from, and the cell number they're assigned. This all happened in the darkness after the prison warden had turned off the lights. At first, I thought that only three prisoners were imprisoned from the clergy, but it became clear that other members of the clergy were also imprisoned. In fact, within one week seven bishops, and twenty-four priests were imprisoned in El-Marg prison, and a few days this number rose to 58.

The next morning, the head of the prison services came to our cell to introduce himself. He apologised to us for our imprisonment and was checking to see if we were comfortable in our cells. He said that our imprisonment was for the peace of the country, and it was only the circumstances that put us in this prison rather than committing any crime. They took us all together in a bus to be questioned by the public prosecutor and I began to wonder, 'why are we being imprisoned if we're innocent of their accusations of treason or rebellion against the government?'

Within the first week, we were given a Bible, Agpia and Psalmodia (midnight praises) book. They permitted us to spend half an hour each day in the prison yard, during which we were given the chance to walk around and breathe some fresh air. Then we would return to be locked up in our cells for the rest of the day.

On the 6th of October 1981, we were told that Bishop Samuel would be coming to visit us at around 2 p.m. We stood outside in the courtyard preparing ourselves as to what we would say and do. Unfortunately, however, Bishop Samuel never came and thus we were escorted back into our cells at around 3 p.m. A little while later, we heard the Quran prayers being broadcasted throughout the prison speakers. Mr. Samir Tadrous, being a man inquisitive by nature, asked the prison guard, "Why is the Quran being broadcast at this hour? What has happened? Has President Sadat died?"

The very next day at 6 a.m., after Bishop Fam and I had finished praying the midnight praises, we heard the voice of the prison guard announcing the arrival of the warden and the prison doors were opened. We were only allowed to listen to the announcement confined in our cells. The announcement was, "visitations have been cancelled for today due to the emergency situation of the assassination of President Sadat." We were expecting to have visitors for the first time on this day, yet the prison gates were shut once again.

We were all shocked by the assassination of President Sadat. Now since he had been killed, who could release us from imprisonment? We thought for a few minutes on the gravity of our situation.

As each prison cell was being locked, a prison guard passed by each cell to see our reaction to the assassination. When the prison guard stood in front of me, I greeted him and said sincerely, "My condolences." However, the prison guard gave a sarcastic smile, probably thinking that I was mocking or gloating about the assassination of Sadat. Later that day, news began to arrive about what had happened in relation to the assassination.

A few days later we were escorted onto buses and travelled to another prison in Wadi El-Natroun. Initially we thought we were being sent to the monastery in Wadi El-Natroun, but we spent a further 35 days in this prison, which was not dissimilar to a maximum-security prison for serious crimes. I used to stay up late at night and saw rats running in the cell and moving across the faces of the fathers while they were sleeping. We eventually returned to El-Marg Prison. In total, I was imprisoned for 341 days.

Throughout the time spent between El-Marg Prison and Wadi El-Natroun, we prayed together with one of the bishops leading the Agpia prayers every day and giving a short sermon. As monks we didn't really mind the imprisonment, but people who were married were more concerned with the safety and wellbeing of their families as no visitations were initially permitted.

Prior to the assassination of President Sadat, we prayed for him every morning that God may grant him safety and wisdom to lead Egypt in peace, especially since at that time the political situation in Egypt was tense.

I can recall a miracle that occurred while we were in prison. We had a priest among us from Sohag, Fr. Maximous, who was from a small town in Boutakh. Unfortunately, Fr. Maximous had severe asthma and trouble breathing. One time when we were returning to our cells, Fr. Maximous asked the prison guard to close the door slowly to allow more air to flow inside. Another prison guard, who had a higher rank, was standing close by and asked the other prison guard what Fr. Maximous had said to him. When the guard told him that Fr Maximous had requested for the door to be closed slowly, he was greatly displeased and rebuked the younger guard saying, "Do we take orders from prisoners now?! Hurry up and close the door quickly!". As the guard was closing the door, the key to rotate the lock broke and thus the guard had to return the door to an unlocked position. The guards called maintenance to try and fix the key and weld it back together. During this time the higher ranked guard personally came to try to shut the door but when he rotated the key in the lock, it broke again leaving the door wide open. Throughout this time the door to the cell remained open allowing Fr. Maximous to breathe easily!

Towards the end of my imprisonment, I witnessed the release of many prisoners, most of whom were laymen and priests. I was the last bishop to be released and the first bishop to be acquitted by a court order. During my stay in prison, I filled six books with many contemplations and sermons, as well as plans for the growth of the diocese! I remained hopeful that I would eventually be released and return to my diocese. We received many visitors who often would break down into tears, but we assured them that everything would return to normal soon. A few of us saw visions of the late Pope Kyrillos VI telling us that this period of tribulation would end soon. Another person had a vision of St. Mary, who also assured him not to worry or fear.

Early on the morning of the assassination of President Sadat, the 6th of October 1981, Fr. Louka Sidarous and Fr. Samuel Thabet were awake in their cell. Fr. Louka heard a voice saying, "The order has been given." He asked Fr. Samuel what he meant, but Fr. Samuel denied saying anything. Fr. Louka answered, "This must have been the voice of God." Certainly, the hand of God becomes more apparent through trials and tribulations, much like the story in the fiery furnace with the three young men when Christ appeared as the face of a man.

On the 26th of July 1982, I was transported to court in a secured cage. There were other prisoners in the same cage with me, some of whom were Muslim, Salafis and extremists. We were talking and laughing together while the news reporters were taking photos of us in the cage. When my name was called out for my case to be heard by the court, my attorney stood up to address the court counsel. He said, "These people are innocent. A disagreement occurred between Pope Shenouda and President Sadat, thus Sadat retaliated by imprisoning Pope Shenouda's children." I remember thinking to myself that the attorney's opening statement sounded quite weak, but I didn't say anything since he was a very experienced attorney. When I was given permission to speak, I said, "Your honour, we are clergymen, and our message is to spread love and peace among people. It is most unfortunate that we are accused of the opposite."

I was silent for a moment while the court counsel prompted me to take my time and continue. I continued, "The accusation that I used to go to small towns on Friday and many people would come to greet me as causing rebellion among the nation and disrupting Muslim prayers is a great misunderstanding. The fact that I was greeted by several Christians and some of our Muslim brothers means that this was not a rebellious act. If I have gone to a town where many Christians are coming to greet me, it is nothing other than love between the congregation and its shepherd. Has love now become a reason to be charged in court?"

As I was speaking, I could see the chief judge leaned to the judge on his left several times. I later learned that the judge on the left was a Christian man named Ramez. In fact, I later visited Ramez in his house after I was exonerated and he told me that when the chief judge leaned towards me during the court hearing, he did not believe that I could be accused of all these crimes. On another occasion the chief judge said, "Your clergymen are very humble and meek." I found his judgment to be very objective.

After I finished addressing all the points regarding the false accusations against me, the court hearing came to an end with the judge exonerating me of all accusations. Despite this, I wasn't released until the ministry of internal affairs approved my discharge on the 7th of August 1982, which was the first day of St Mary's fast. Additionally, I wasn't allowed to immediately return to my diocese after my release, thus I was exiled from my diocese in total for about 40 months.

PRAYERS THAT SHOOK
THE PRISON WALLS

FR BOULES BASILI

In the district of El-Marg stood a prison that I never would have imagined being imprisoned in, let alone seeing. I experienced solitary confinement, where all prisoners are first introduced to receive 'the greatest of trials.'

It was a memorable day that I will never forget when Sadat ordered, or more correctly when the investigators of national security ordered, us to be sent into the depths of the prison. The national security would falsely accuse a Christian with any form of treason which they could invoke and send to prison without having a conviction.

It turned out that I was spending the summer of 1981 at home in the district of Abu Keer when on Thursday the 3rd September 1981, uninvited guests came knocking violently at my home ordering me to get dressed and be accompanied to the police station. The guards recognised me from work as they were from parliament house, and then they took me down to the police station in Alexandria.

I asked the officer: "Why I am under arrest?"

The officer answered me: "We really don't know"

I said to him: "It better not be about El Shaarawy?!" 5

The Officer said: "Probably it is, but regardless, it will only be a few minutes from your time, then you're free to go!"

I said to him: "So I don't have to bring with me a bag or anything?"

He answered: "No, there's no need".

I put on my clothes and followed the officers until the sight downstairs took me by surprise where there was an army van filled with soldiers accompanied with police officers. Two police officers grabbed me from each arm and tried to push me into the backseat of the van. I resisted; thus, they took me to the front seat where I was squashed between two police officers.

I waited for the general constable for four hours that morning. It occurred to me that they had obviously lied to me about the reason for transporting me to the police station when they arrested me. When I needed to use the bathroom, I was accompanied by three police officers who stood outside my cubicle. What was happening?! They did not even leave me alone to use the bathroom?! Finally, at around 10 a.m. I was given orders to move down to the street.

5 Sharawy was a Sheikh of El Azhaar who had been causing religious unrest because of his blatant encouragement of anti-Christian sentiment in his Friday sermons publicly broadcasted.

At the door of the police station, I heard one policeman call out for handcuffs. Another officer eagerly came forward and tried to put the handcuffs on me. I resisted and said, "Handcuffs?! Why, am I a criminal?!" However, I accepted what God gave me and co-operated with the police officers to be handcuffed as I considered myself worthy to endure pain for the sake of Christ! The policeman looked at me with guilt in his eyes and said to me, "I am sorry, Father, but we must follow through with these orders."

They put me inside an army van again, surrounded by a multitude of soldiers, policemen and detectives and the car drove off through the crowd. A lot of people after discovering this news stood around to watch, including five cars filled with soldiers and policemen. If it wasn't for the war of October 1973 which had already ended, I would have thought that we were going to fight the Israelites. I was deeply ashamed when I was driven through the crowd of people surrounding the van hearing them shout out, "Look at the criminals!"

I leaned forward to a soldier sitting next to me and asked him, "where are we were going?". He said, "I do not know, but it is not just you. It has been two days and we have been arresting people like you". It turns out that I was not the first priest to be arrested. As we drove by, I saw the gates of a large government building with high walls and a large sign, 'El-Marg Prison'. I also saw firsthand a multitude of priests dressed in their black garments present.

I was glad it was a prison in the surrounding city rather and a remote prison in the desert or mountain!

After an hour had passed when we had arrived, I was fully striped searched and a police officer had the following conversations with me:

"Are you Boules Basili?"

"No, I am Father Boules Basili"

"What does Father mean?"

"It means a priest, as mentioned in the Qur'an"

"Well, you know the Qur'an, why then did they bring you here?"

"Maybe because I know the Qur'an!"

We both laughed, along with a few other policemen! As I entered the gates of the prison, I was welcomed by a tall solid man with a physique that was reminiscent of Samson in the bible, except he had an evil facial look. He smiled at me and grabbed my arm aggressively calling out, "Open cell 11". Believe me, dear reader, when I tell you that I have never entered a prison, let alone a police station in my entire life. I also will take this opportunity to tell everyone who has never visited prison to do so voluntarily while they still have the chance, to understand what truly happens inside.

I remember a journalist named Samir Tadrous who had been imprisoned more than once for political reasons and would have gladly walk back into prison with a smile on his face. He actually seemed to enjoy spending time in prison. Samir was a leader among prisoners and would see new prisoner arrivals from where he was sitting calling out to everyone, "Hello, we now have a new arrival to our prison. Father _____ from such place has entered cell number _____. Please introduce yourself when you have settled in your cell." After several hours, we heard the new prisoner call out his name, job/status, and the crime apparently committed!

The prison was humid in the hot month of September, especially ٦٦٦when you lay down on concrete floors staring up at reinforced concrete roofs! I will not lie; my cell number 11 was a lucky cell. Firstly, I was lucky because my cell was on the eastern side, allowing a cool breeze to enter from the 10 cm window, and secondly my cellmate was another priest named Fr. Basilious Sidrac who had previously served in San Louis in America. He had a good sense of humour and never left a chance to make a joke whenever possible. He made it easier for me to bear the cross of my imprisonment. I will take an opportunity to recount one of his jokes.

When the chief prison guard wanted to introduce himself to the 'new prisoners' he would go and meet them in their cells. I first introduced myself as Fr. Boules Basili, while the chief prison guard responded, "Welcome!" I did not know whether by him saying 'welcome' he was genuine or sarcastic, but in any case, when it was the turn of my cellmate to introduce himself, he said he was Fr. Basilious from El Menia – and here I should mention that he was quite tall in height – and the chief guard said, "Ah yes you are with Bishop Beimen, right?", "No, actually, another Bishop named Arsanius." Thus, the prison guard asked, "Well, why isn't he here with us?" to which Fr. Basilious answered quickly, "because he is very short, and I am twice his height. The policemen choose prisoners according to their height, so they took me instead of him!" The chief prison guard and other guards laughed, and since that time they repeated this joke to others for a laugh.

I was truly lucky that Fr. Basilious was tall and could breathe in the good air from the little window, while it didn't matter that I lay flat on my face to breathe in the toxic air from under the door. The first night I spent in prison was quite a life changing experience. It changes your state of freedom into a life of strenuous exile and imprisonment. This night, on the 3rd of September 1981, was one of the worst nights of my life. When the policeman took me to my cell 11, it was occupied temporarily, thus I was placed in cell 10. As I walked in, I saw two laymen sitting down, and I recognised one of them, Deacon Abdel Messih, who was patting the back of the other who was crying. He was not familiar to me, but he later introduced himself as Mr. Phillip, who was a principal of a school in Assiut. He was crying bitterly, and I thought to myself, why is he crying? Did they viciously beat him up?!

Deacon Abdel Messih told me that Mr. Phillip was crying because his wife and kids did not know where he was. I told him, "Today is Thursday and tomorrow Friday so they will not open up a file. You will just have to wait till Saturday and then they will let you go!" Mr. Phillip became more upset saying, "This means I have to wait three more days?!" Obviously, Mr. Phillip did not want to spend a long time in prison, let alone for three days! Yet in fact, he ended up being imprisoned for several months! Whenever I saw Mr. Phillip, I would say to him, "You couldn't wait only three days?!"

Darkness fell that night on the 3rd September like I have never experienced before. The narrow window in the cell did not permit any rays of light so that I couldn't even see the toilet seat. The toilet seat was just an opening in the floor 70 cm by 70 cm. My cellmate, Fr. Basilious, was a large man that required my assistance to use the toilet. I had to support him like a wall. The toilet was not connected to a flush, so the stench would fill the prisons very quickly for an extended amount of time. May God forgive the people who were behind such punishment!

After the release of Bishop Beimen from prison, may God rest his soul, he was asked by his congregation where he had been. He responded jokingly, "I was in a Sheraton 5-star hotel!" The truth is that the beds to sleep on were simply mats no more than 1 cm thick and were placed directly on the uneven concrete floor. The roof was made of reinforced concrete that directed heat inside the cells, particularly during summer when the sweltering heat was unbearable.

In relation to our food in prison, we were handed plates of food to eat each day. One was a plate of lentils, which was filled with little pebbles and rocks. The other was a plate of baked beans, which was filled with cockroaches – both dead and alive. We had to confer with the bishops imprisoned as to whether this food was really breaking our fast, given that it was filled with cockroaches! The only other plate offered to us was a plate of white cheese that did not have any fat whatsoever, donated to us by the chief guard. We had to leave the cheese in a cup of water to dissolve a bit and moisten, in order to be able to eat it.

My diabetes flared up dangerously during my stay in the prison. I reached a level of 520 mg/dl of blood sugar level, and acetone spread around my body to the extent that H.G. Bishop Bishoy of Dumyat commented, "I used to be able to smell the acetone in your breath!". The attending prison doctor Magdy El Desouky unintentionally gave me an expired box of test strips for my blood sugar level. When I tested my sugar level and found no change, I kept eating normally. Due to my high blood sugar level, I lost consciousness in the prison hall and was transported to the emergency ward set aside for prison inmates. When I was carried off into the ambulance, eight bishops and 23 priests all stood up in prison and offered fervent prayers for my sake, interceding that God may grant me a full recovery. In total I spent ten days in rehabilitation. I remember my friend Sheikh Mahlawy, the preacher from the Ibrahim Basha Mosque, who was in the room next to me getting upset from the amount of phone calls regarding my condition. The prison even received calls from the department of internal affairs asking, "How is Fr. Boules?" They didn't really care about me but rather were worried that I might die and word would spread that the prison had killed a Coptic priest. This was in light of the fact that a few days earlier the former minister Abdel Azeem Abu-el-Atta had passed away, which could have raised concern! One should note that Sheikh Mahlawy was the person whom President Sadat had spoken about saying, "He is thrown in prison like a dog!"

After I was released from prison on 28th April 1982, I went with my wife to the monastery of St. Bishoy to take the blessing of H.H. Pope Shenouda and to ask about his health. I will not forget what H.H said to me that day: "Fr. Boules, I used to remember you every day in my prayers when you were in the hospital. Thank God for your recovery!"

Later when I visited my children in America in June 1982, I found out that the church had fasted for three days a week (Wednesday-Friday) for H.H Pope Shenouda and the other prisoners. This fasting continued until our imprisonment had ended, demonstrating the loyalty of the congregation who offered selfless service on our behalf.

We were later transported to another prison in Wadi El Natroun because the guards feared for our safety. El-Marg prison became unsafe due to the presence of extremists who had been sentenced to this prison. During our stay, a Christian police officer was murdered by one of those extremists, thus they thought of transferring us to Wadi El Natroun for our own protection. We were transported in two prison buses in the middle of the night unaware of where we were going. Finally, we found ourselves in front of a very large sign that said, 'Wadi El Natroun Prison'. In all honesty, the prison in Wadi El Natroun was more comfortable than El-Marg prison as at least we could sleep on metal bunk beds.

After two days of settling in this prison, the general lieutenant of prison affairs of Cairo came and visited us. When he got to our door, he saw us standing up in prayer and waited in the administration office until we finished praying. Shortly after he greeted us very warmly and extended this courtesy to all the other prisoners. When he us asked if we had any questions, a layman asked him, "When are we going to be set free?" He quickly responded, "Believe me, my son, I don't know. I have no information in this matter. However, when I came, I saw you praying... keep praying that the situation will be resolved!" His words seemed to have had a hidden meaning as President Sadat was killed just 30 days after our incarceration.

Further memories of the past include an astonishing account of our prayer life in prison. We started praying the seven hourly prayers every day from the day we were incarcerated. After finishing the morning prayer, we performed four hundred prostrations saying 'Lord have mercy' (Keyrie Leison in Greek) in one echoing voice! Our utterance of these words used to shake the prison walls to the extent that one of the officials came asking, "What are you saying?! The prison is shaking... what is this 'sound' you keep making?!" We explained to him that Keyrie Leison is a Greek prayer of two words; Keyrie meaning 'O' Lord' and Leison meaning 'Have Mercy'. He replied saying: "Well then He did have mercy already", referring to the death of Sadat that was truly unexpected. Though we replied, "No, not yet.", He replied smiling, "I'm just scared for myself now!" and as he was leaving, "Well, try to take it easy. I feel that the prison is going to collapse from all the shaking!"

There is a saying that behind every great man, there's a great woman. I can hardly call myself great, however, I can proudly call my wife great. Before I was arrested, I left my wife to take care of her sister who was diagnosed with cancer while I went to take a break in Abu Keer. I certainly did not intend for this break to extend into an imprisonment, but this is exactly what happened!

My wife was in her father's house when the guards came early in the morning and asked her to accompany them to our house. My wife took her brother along with her and as she approached our street, she saw that both sides of the street were full of police officers and security cars. My wife's strong faith allowed her to endure the police entering the house and tear the house apart searching for something. She asked them what they were looking for and they said "weapons"!

My wife took the police officers into the foyer of the house, where a large marble cross hung on the wall. The police said, "This is our weapon", and they persisted to search for something else. After a while, one of the police officers called out, "I found it!" holding in his hands some of the lectures and recordings that I had made defending Christian dogma! My wife said, "Are you looking for the recordings? Come, I will show you all of them!" and she pulled out a carton box which contained about 180 recorded cassettes, which they confiscated.

Many questions began to arise from the congregation concerning the numerous arrests of the clergy and laity, including why Fr. Boulous was imprisoned? After all, Fr. Boulous held distinctive positions; he was a key member of Parliament, the press editor-in-chief, a theological college seminary professor and the leader of national unity in Shubra, among many other important positions. What crime had he committed?! Why would they arrest him? He was a peacemaker to the unruly angry mob that revolted and protested against Islamic extremists who labelled Christians as atheists and insulted them. Fr. Boulous became the official leader of national unity in Shubra, working at calming the anger arisen between Muslims and Christians through utmost respect and calmness. Fr. Boulous found verses from the Quran that defended the Lord Jesus Christ, which is the greatest testimony of the good character and peacefulness of the Christian faith. An axiom said by the late Saad Zaghloul complemented this situation, "Before you tell the person to stop crying, tell the person to stop attacking". In other words, Fr. Boulos left the instigator to continue attacking and this was considered a rebellious act, thus Fr. Boulous was unlawfully imprisoned.

It may have been justifiable to accuse only one person of an alleged rebellious crime, yet the police imprisoned the Pope, eight bishops and 24 priests, among dozens of laymen and high-ranking citizens. This number of arrests to the clergy and laity set a new precedent. They were transferred into prison like dangerous criminals!

A book written by Anwar Mohammed titled 'Sadat and the Pope' indicates the tension between the government and the church, which led president Sadat to issue a warrant for the imprisonment of the Pope along with eight bishops and 24 priests in a 'safe place'! Along with this arrest warrant, Sadat issued a warrant to foreclose 13 charitable committees, including an association called "El Karma" for the blind. I was utterly surprised at this decision since the association was run by Mrs. Gihan El Sadat, the wife of the president, yet even this did not stop him from deciding to close it.

We would like to shed some light on the circumstances of the prison by sharing what Dr. Milad Hanna wrote in a unique way. We heard him say, "In the time where the prison cell could hardly fit one person, more prisoners were being added each day!". Prisoners came in large groups of varying ranks of priesthood and occupation, while we were forced to squeeze three prisoners into each cell! Sleep was becoming almost impossible to achieve, and even turning from side to side required asking permission from another cellmate. This reminded me of cooking chicken sticks on a fire. I also thought of the violation of human rights that arose from our treatment! The strong stench of sweat and the sewerage system was psychologically and physically overwhelming throughout my stay in prison. The cracks in the walls of the cells resulted in an innumerable number of cockroaches, ants and other disgusting insects being present inside! The sound of a mosquito flying by your ear was irritating and its sting aggravated the situation making it very difficult to sleep at all. When I asked the accompanying guard Abdel-Ghani, "why are there so many mosquitos"? He responding saying, "because we are close to the sewerage pipes that lead to the Yellow Mountain."

In the morning, the young men that worked in the prison came with old bins that I previously saw being used to collect garbage in poor districts. The stench of rotten oil would even spread to your nostrils. The food that we ate was stored inside these bins, while the bread was cold enough to remind us of the sinking feeling we had deep inside of us!

Another prison guard would come and distribute white cheese to the inmates using his dirty hands. We received a piece of cheese on bread and started devouring our food. We stopped complaining about our hunger and got used to the darkness inside our cells. We also came to realise and accept that our food was infested with 'proteins' that came from dead bugs and live worms, yet we ate anyway! At lunchtime we would often eat lentils, which later turned out to be an invaluable meal as it became food for the wealthy in the midst of a famine in Egypt.

I remember the story of Bishop Samuel who used to visit my wife and kids to try and comfort them. He told them that I'm not living in prison but rather in a palace of one of the presidential lineages in the district called El-Marg. Bishop Samuel would encourage my wife and tell her stories of how I would tend the prison garden with the help of other bishops, all enjoying our time together in happiness and joy! My wife regained hope when she learned that Bishop Samuel's assistant would visit me in my 'palace' everyday! She believed in the faith and optimism of Bishop Samuel.

The government was at least honest in keeping us in a 'safe place', thus we did not mind the 'vacation'. We were able to not only endure but enjoy it!

On Wednesday 14th October 1981, we were surprised to hear that we had to pack up and leave the prison. Our simple hearts thought that we were being released, while our cynical thoughts began to think of worst-case scenarios. Some thought that we were being transported to another prison due to fear of our lives. We quietly and diligently walked out of the El-Marg prison, which became an emotional experience. The moment we stepped out of prison we were swamped with armed police officers. We were pushed into vans which were dark and lacked any windows for ventilation. We were shoved into these vans and everyone scrambled around for a place to stand or hold onto. We were swung dangerously with every movement of the van. Despite this ordeal, we were still happy that we could all be bonded together.

All the prisoners eventually reached the prison in Wadi El Natroun where we were packed into a wide room filled with rats and roaches and a very dirty toilet. However, despite the horrid stench we still could maintain our happiness.

We saw a few familiar faces in the prison of Wadi El Natroun, including Bishop Benjamin of El Menofeya and the late Bishop Beimen of Malawy. Also, in the prison was Metropolitan Bishoy of Dumyat, Bishop Fam of Temma who was only ordained a bishop a few months earlier, along with Bishop Wissa of El-Balina and Bishop Ammonious of Luxor. Other bishops included Bishop Bemwa, who seemed to know nothing regarding politics. The latest addition to the prison was Bishop Tadrous of Port Said, who was in Cyprus on a mission trip when he found out that there was a warrant for his arrest. He wanted to return to Egypt to be persecuted with the people of God rather than to stay in Cyprus or escape to America, despite even his family and friends trying to convince him to flee to America to escape arrest. This story was recounted by our own beloved hegumen Fr. Bishoy Ghobrial!

An amusing story arose from one of the laymen who was

imprisoned with us, journalist Sameer Tadrous, who chose the first cell in prison close to the prison gates. He used to converse with our friend Dr. Milad Hanna and they would delve into heated discussions about politics, which was a great comfort and entertainment in our struggle! There was a continuous conversation between prison cell 1 and cell 8 about politics. I will never forget Dr. Milad Hanna who was wrongly imprisoned. Being a loud politician, he was quickly transferred to a group of politicians who were in trouble just like him.

As we mention memories from prison life, we also cannot forget the tremendous effort from the ladies who served us while we were imprisoned. This group of wonderful servants used to cook for us and send food when the guards allowed us to eat from it. They sent fruits, peanuts and even lollipops! It was as if we were their children being catered by our mothers! May God bless these Coptic women!

We also cannot forget the tireless efforts of Mr. Gerges who was the episcopal service delegate and secretary for Bishop Samuel who was martyred. He used to visit us daily in prison and then visit our families, reassuring them of our own wellbeing.

Effectively the prison turned into a church and theological college through us. It was my duty to give sermons daily, while Metropolitan Bishoy, along with the late Bishop Beimen and Rev.

Father Tadrous, used to give bible studies. Bishop Fam would teach the midnight praises, while Rev. Father Ibrahim Abdo would give hymn lessons. Bishop Benjamin, Bishop Tadrous, Bishop Ammonious and Bishop Bemwa used to share in giving sermons and teachings. Rev. Fr. Zachariah Botrous used to sew and fix our clothes with just a needle and he used to attach the prisoner numbers on their clothes as a service.

What was truly amazing and unforgettable was that we prayed liturgies on the feasts of Nativity and Epiphany. These liturgies were truly remarkable with eight bishops, 24 priests and over a hundred deacons attending! What was even more astonishing was that we ordained two new deacons; Dr. Nabil from Sohag, and Mr. Abdel-Masih Baseet (currently Father Abdel-Masih in Mostorod). We also celebrated the birth of children to both Fr. Samuel Thabet and Fr. Ibrahim Abdo respectively. The mothers brought their children into prison and we ordained them, celebrating with candles and prayers while congratulating both families.

One of the unforgettable miracles that occurred during our imprisonment was the healing of a prisoner's burnt hands while he was working with the kitchen oven. The doctors decided to amputate his arms, but the priests and bishops insisted to wait and give God a chance to heal him. We had seven of the best doctors in our midst; including surgeon Dr. Helmy El-Gohary.

We asked them to pay a lot of attention to the injured prisoner, and truly God granted this man a speedy recovery. The healed prisoner shouted saying, "I want to be like you! I want to be one of you!"

The cruelty of the prison guards reached a shameful level, as for instance they prevented me from receiving a suitcase of clothes which my wife sent while I was imprisoned. When Bishop Benjamin found out that I had no clothes, he came and gave me a costly gown which he received from his congregation while he was imprisoned. I was ashamed to accept his clothes and felt unworthy, especially when I had to be transferred to the prison in Wadi El Natroun. When I was transferred, I reclaimed my suitcase of clothes and eventually returned the gown back to Bishop Benjamin personally thanking him.

Bishop Tadrous was a pharmacist administering my medications. He received medications from a pharmacy belonging to Dr. Adel in Port Said. Bishop Ammonious and Bishop Bemwa were both so kind to me and used to leave me their portion of meat or chicken in the corner of my cell, largely out of mercy towards my sickness. Also, Bishop Fam would lead midnight praises every night which used to calm us down and ease our pains and illnesses.

In terms of our meals, Bishop Wissa would take charge and

line us up to receive our daily portion of food. When it came to desserts, Metropolitan Bishoy took charge of distributing the portions and would always give me a smaller portion saying, "You only receive a small piece 1 cm by 1 cm!" He did this for fear of what affect sugar might have on my health.

After we had spent a period in Wadi El Natroun, we were finally transferred back to our original prison in El-Marg. However, this time we were met with more pleasant treatment from the prison guard looking after us. We found out that the wife of this prison guard was a doctor and that she had several friends who were Christian doctors. They had warned her about the harsh treatment her husband executed towards Christian prisoners. She said to her husband, "Mahmoud, you have to treat those Christians with the respect they deserve otherwise they might pray against our children as they prayed against El-Sadat, and you saw what happened to him! We only have two children, I'm begging you!"

Mahmoud visited us in prison every day and asked if he had done anything to upset anyone or said something to annoy us in any way. He used to say that his wife kept nagging him every day to respect those Christians. It got to the point that once Mahmoud brought his two children to prison for us to pray over them. Truly he was a noble person!

Upon the completion of our prison sentence, the prison officer said to us: "You've transformed my standard of behaviour as a prison guard! I cannot swear, hit or abuse anyone anymore. This is the key to being a good prison guard!" We later found out that he took vacation for a year without pay and began a small business. Thus, we realised that we had become missionaries even in prison, fulfilling the command of St. Paul who said, "Be ready in season and out of season. Convince, rebuke, exhort, with all longsuffering and teaching." (2 Tim 4: 2)

We also remember Dr. Milad Hanna who was forcedly imprisoned for being mistaken as a revolutionist, although he was just very passionate about politics. His presence with us was a blessing and made prison life more bearable. He did not fear anyone, as demonstrated once when we heard him angrily screaming and shouting against Sadat and the government representatives. Subsequently we feared that we would be mistreated even more, especially since we didn't know that the prison was tapped with listening devices. Shortly after, we witnessed government leaders in authority showing up in prison and transporting Dr. Milad for interrogation. He refused to deny what he said about the president, and thus was punished by being placed in the 'Trial cell', known as the being the most severe place in prison. A few days after this incident, we heard of the president's assassination on the podium and simply said, "May he rest in peace", for we were taught by Christ Himself to "love your enemies, bless those who curse you, do good to those who hate you, and pray for those who spitefully use you and persecute you" (Matt 5: 44).

We developed friendships with many of the police chiefs, among whom was Lieutenant Ragab Abdel-Hamid who visited us every time he travelled to Shobra. Lieutenant Ragab visited me late in 1980 and invited me into his office, politely asking me to stop responding towards Sheikh El-Shaarawy. Lieutenant Ragab accused me of causing sectarian strife among Christians and Muslims. I remember telling him, "Lieutenant Ragab, I want you to remember the saying of Saad Zaghloul who said 'Before you tell the person to stop crying, tell the person to stop attacking', and the colloquial idiom that says, 'you let go first, then I'll let go!" Thus, before you ask me to stop responding, tell them to stop attacking! The television makes false accusations against our doctrines and I cannot stand by silently. Our responses came as a series of lectures that were directly taken and quoted from Quranic verses. The popular proverb says, "Whoever is silent about the truth is a mute devil!". Lieutenant Ragab smiled at me and said, "a master of silence is wiser than him who speaks."

Truly, we had the utmost honour to be imprisoned as we believed that we were like the apostles and the prophets, whom St Paul writes about saying, "Still others had trials of mocking and scourging, yes, and of chains and imprisonment.

They were stoned, they were sawn in two, were tempted, and were slain with the sword. They wandered about in sheepskins and goatskins, being destitute, afflicted, tormented" (Heb 11: 36-37).

The public prosecutor interrogated us for five and a half hours consecutively and his report filled nearly 55 pages. He analysed the statements with utmost scrutiny, and in the end, he only could pronounce two words: "NOT GUILTY". Despite the not guilty verdict, I was not released for over a month later. He insisted that I be returned to my cell, lying on the bare cemented floors. I was in agony during this time because of my diabetes which flared up due to lack of treatment. The treatment I received in prison was more harmful than diabetes itself!

During the interrogation of the prosecutor, I realised that he was trying to get me to criticise our beloved Pope Shenouda for his decision to move me from my church in Mesra to El-Wogooh. He was asking me, "So why has your pope moved you from the biggest church to the smallest church in Shubra?" I answered, "This is advantageous for the church in El-Wogooh because the two priests serving there are very old and cannot carry the burden of the service on their own, thus the Pope believed that it would be fitting for me to go there and help carry their responsibilities. It is the same in war, if the captain sees a soldier fatally weak and incapacitated, he would shift soldiers around to protect and assist him. Every half an hour he returned to the same topic to try and get me to criticise Pope Shenouda, but he failed miserably. When he was exhausted, he finally granted me the verdict of "NOT GUILTY".

One time, I fell into a diabetic coma and was taken to Qasr El Eyni hospital and placed in a special ward with guards. I was transported into the recovery room and stayed there for ten days until I finally woke up, not feeling anything or knowing where I was. When I regained consciousness, I was bombarded with a large group of faithful servants visiting me. Many bishops visited me that were delegated by H.H, and other priests visited from Upper Egypt, El-Beheira and Cairo. Students in the hospital also came to visit me, along with members of the People's Assembly, the Senate, and members of charitable organisations including 'El-Karma'. I remember one of the high ranked police detectives visiting and telling me, "You look fine, and your health is getting better. What's wrong with you! Do you want to avoid your conviction sentence?!" My wife, aching, said, "Sir, how can he when you are here?"

Buses full of people came to visit me, as if they were going on a trip or an excursion to the monastery. They struck havoc in the corridors of the hospitals and this alerted the chief manager of the ward, Dr. Hashem Foad. When Dr. Foad found out about my situation, he insisted on visiting me with a group of his fellow doctors to speak about religious matters.

My colleagues Shiek El-Mahlawy, Shiek Koshk and Shiek El-Talmasany frequently visited me. They insisted on visiting me after discovering my deteriorating health. I confess that I had a special friendship with Shiek El-Mahlawy, and countless conversations with him over topics such as backgammon continued even after I was released from prison.

At times the prison was unbearable, though we used to enjoy the company of the prison guards. One of the prison guards, Abdel-Ghani, said to us once, "I see you sitting down and telling jokes, do you want me to tell you a story?" We agreed and he said, "one time a disabled man wanted to get a job in one of the prisons, thus they interviewed him. He was asked a simple set of questions, such as 'where are your eyes?' He then pointed to his mouth. 'Where are your ears?' He pointed to his nose. 'Where are your hands?' He pointed to his head. They gave him a sample question-answer sheet and told him to study it and come back for another test. When he came back, they asked him the exact same questions and he responded in the same manner. They were convinced that he was fit for the job, yet one of the examiners asked him, 'How did you learn all of these answers?' He said, 'from my head' and he pointed to the back of his head!"

Our relationship between the prisoners did not deteriorate

after our return to El-Marg prison from Leiman, but on the contrary grew stronger. We used to sit with Rev. Fr. Tadrous Yacoub, who engaged us in his translation of the writings of the early church fathers. He's truly a great and holy man and very learned in church writings. Rev. Fr. Louka Sidarous and Rev. Fr. Samuel Thabet were disciples of the late Fr. Bishoy Kamel and we experienced great companionship and friendship. I cannot travel to America without first visiting those two wonderful priests. I also remember Fr. Louka who was very knowledgeable in all facets of science and possibly even backgammon! I remember once that Rev. Fr. Sarabamoun, Rev. Fr. Ibrahim, Rev. Fr. Athanasius and I tried to compete against him in a game of backgammon – four against one – and we could not win even once! We joked that he was better in backgammon than his other services as a priest!

Our colleague Rev. Fr. Youssef Assad from El-Omraneya was such a sweet presence among us, and we were blessed to have him with us. I remember that one day Fr. Youssef asked one of his servants to bring him a video camera. Our dear reader, bringing in a video camera into prison is a major felony. This act could lead to incarcerating and punishing the person who smuggled in the camera or the person caught in possession of it! Furthermore, the news of smuggling a camera into prison reached the prison chief, who called and interrogated Fr. Youssef. We feared for his life and fervently prayed for his safety as they might severely harm him, and we tried defend Fr. Youssef to Ommaney the other prison guards in support of his innocence. His reason for bringing in a video camera was merely to capture a glimpse of the valuable moments of history we were witnessing. These simple words were sufficient to soften the heart of the prison chief, who amazingly let him go without any further harm or punishment!

Prior to my arrival to El-Kasr El-Einy, Rev. Fr. Samuel had previously experienced severe pain with kidney failure and was placed in an isolated room. According to the late Bishop Beimen, this room was the equivalent of a five-star hotel! Rev. Fr. Samuel always diligent in keeping his room very neat and organised, and was a truly kind person who was loved by everyone including the late Sheik El-Talmasani who Fr. Samuel often witnessed to.

After my admission to hospital, I was quickly joined by Rev. Fr. Zachariah Boutros and Rev. Fr. Sarabamoun Abdo. They were a great company to have in hospital and they eased my pain greatly. Rev. Fr. Sarabamoun was intelligent and had a simple heart, while Rev. Fr. Zachariah was my roommate in the rehabilitation ward. His presence was a great blessing where we used to spend our time talking and we became very close friends. In fact, our friendship still holds strong till this day. Rev. Fr. Zachariah is a man who has experienced and endured great pain, waiting patiently in the midst of tribulations and persecution. He's a talented speaker and was the prison's tailor, who helped sew our numbers on the prison clothes. We truly missed him after he was forcibly transferred to serve in Australia. How lucky was Australia by his presence, and how unlucky we were in Egypt to have lost him?!

Other supporting fathers among our presence included Rev. Fr. Athanasius Boutros, who was also a great companion in our troubles. Also, I will never forget Rev. Fr. Ibrahim Abdo, who used to teach the Christian prisoners the melodious hymns and praises. We were saddened for him because of his painful back, but he came out of prison healed as he mentioned to us that Pope Kyrillos VI visited him in prison and healed him!

Rev. Fr. Bishoy Yassa, servant in Masr El-Gedida and Madinet-Nasr, was the icon of the faithful servant to us and especially to the late Bishop Beimen, who was ill with various diseases. Fr. Bishoy was his personal assistant and it was like he was closer to him than his own shadow! I was unaware of the numerous virtues Fr. Bishoy had until I lived with him in prison. Blessed are the times of tribulations that put us through fire to purify and show the good characters within us!

I previously mentioned my wife's courage when facing some of the police officers who went to my house and started questioning her about alleged crimes committed. I recall that she came every day while I was in hospital and bring food. She woke up early every day to cook and bring the food with her. She was harassed each time she passed through security guards allocated on ward 14, where I was being held. The guards were truly rude and annoying, yet she went through this ordeal every day for me.

I will not forget the one time that my wife and Rev. Fr. Samuel Thabet had to wait three hours for the guards to allow them just to visit me. I also remember the wife of one of the other prisoners who used to drive down from Alexandria every day to visit her husband. I couldn't imagine how tired she would have been just from driving, let alone go through the trouble of having to wait for the guards to let her inside!

How can I forget my children (Francoise, Samir and Farid) who came from America to visit me? I also remember my brother Fawzy, who used to exhaust himself to visit me and take articles that I wrote to try and prove my innocence regarding the accusations against me. His work availed much, for his voice reached the 'People's Assembly'! I also remember my beloved son Dr. Lamey Asham-Allah who used to call journalists and chief executives to try and prove my innocence. He is one of the most honest and trustworthy men that I have ever known and he still serves his country in the matter of the 'National issue'.

I was extraordinarily successful in obtaining a seat in the 'People's Assembly' against my opponent who was a millionaire Muslim mayor. However, I was faced with rebutting campaigns that accused me of forsaking the church and altar, and my service as a priest, to become a political advocate and member of the government.

God knows that even when I was standing on the parliament podium, I never once forgot my church but voiced my opinion as loudly as I could about the rights of Copts. I brought to everybody's attention the difficulties in freeing the churches from oppression. It got to a stage that the previous vice-president Mamdouh Salem complained to Mayor Albert Barsoum Salama about me. Mamdous Salem claimed that I voiced the existence of church oppression in the parliament house, which made the government look ashamed. Despite my vocal disagreement to this law, it fell on deaf ears. I kept voicing my opinion until the last day of my membership in parliament. To this day I still voice my opinion because I believe "whoever is silent about the truth is a mute devil!".

Despite my efforts to clear my name as a rebel, I was labelled 'the priest from parliament'. Shortly after the morning of Thursday 3rd of September 1981, I was arrested and imprisoned. By now, the government was imprisoning any member of the government without any justifiable cause or reason. Only when my innocence became clear to everybody, that the prosecutors began to realise that I was mistaken for a government agent. They realised that I was an honest and courageous man who only voiced his outrage against an ancient and misunderstood law that ought to be revoked.

After spending nine months in prison and hospital, the day of my release finally came. It is common protocol that whoever is released from prison must first meet with the chief detective. On the 28th April 1982, it was my turn to meet with Detective Aita, who was indeed polite and well-mannered. He greeted me warmly with a smile and sincere embrace, saying:

"Excuse us, father. I honestly listened to all of your tapes over four hours and I could not find one single word that attacked anybody."

I asked him, "Then why did you imprison me, an elderly and sick man, and why did you leave others free who attacked and mocked people?"

He smiled politely, and said, "Excuse us, father, it is a political issue. Just as we took Sheikh Koshk, we had to take Rev. Fr. Boulos".

I replied, "But did you hear what Sheikh Koshk said about

President Sadat? How he insulted him and his lineage and called his wife the 'indecent woman of Egypt'?"

He replied, "Excuse us again, father, it was a situation that has finally passed and you are a faithful person. Do not be upset. In truth, we can never forget your voice amid the People's Assembly." These simple words left a serene thought in my mind and I came out of prison stronger than when I went in... thanks be to God!

REV FATHER BOULOS CONCLUDES, SAYING:

One of the many benefits I gained from my imprisonment was that, through God's grace, I was able to write and subsequently publish four books. The first book titled 'Copts; national and historical', was reprinted three times in the first year of its publication. The second titled 'The model podium', the third 'I can do all things', and the fourth 'My memoirs in half a century', which is in your hands, dear reader.

In truth, these nine months that we spent inside prison will never be forgotten. We learned many valuable lessons:

1. We learned that God is with us, "If God is for us, who can be against us" (Rom 8:31).

2. We learned that God is just and fair, for after exactly thirty days our gracious God dealt justly against our prosecutor.

3. We learned patience, for "by your patience possesses your souls" (Lk 21:19).

4. We learned that even in prison it is "good and pleasant for brethren to dwell together in unity. It is like the precious oil upon the head, running down on the beard, the beard of Aaron, running down on the edge of his garments.... For there the Lord commanded blessing!" (Ps 133:1-3)

5. We learned that our bishops and priests bore their crosses with thanksgiving, pride and patience.

6. We learned how to be role models and to fulfil the commandment of the Lord who said, "Let your light so shine before men, that they may see your good works and glorify your Father in heaven." (Mt 5:16)

The prison guards also confided in us that we were different to other prisoners. In fact, the guards became upset when they heard that a group of us was being released and that they would not be able to spend any more time with us. We used to keep the guard's company and ease their sorrow and troubles, as much as we could from prison.

Truly, ever since the new president Mohamad Hosny Mubarak took charge of the situation, he began to release us from prison. It started by issuing an order to ease our imprisonment that allowed our families to visit us. Colonel Mahmoud El-Gameel opened his own office for visits from our wives and relatives. He was truly a great man and treated us very well.

In November 1981 the order was issued to release the first group of laymen from prison. This was great news to us and it calmed our souls greatly. When we celebrated New Year's Eve at church following our release it was truly a magnificent and unforgettable night that continued until dawn! It was filled with prayers, singing, psalms and hymns led by eight bishops and twenty-four priests.

I also should mention a time in prison when my left leg was in danger of being amputated due to poorly managing my diabetes. I battled this medical condition for several months in prison, and at one stage the leg turned bright red, a critical situation. Metropolitan Bishoy confessed that he personally cared for me until my leg recovered without requiring any amputation.

PRIOR TO OUR RELEASE

It was decided that on the 25th April 1982 the Israeli soldiers would withdraw from the Sinai Peninsula. However, the Israeli negotiator was cunning and threatened to cancel the peace treaty, saying that there was incomplete normalisation between the Egyptian and Israeli people (normalisation was one of the conditions for the peace treaty). This negotiator highlighted the fact that Egyptians were banned from visiting Israel. Effectively, President Anwar Sadat gambled with all his political chips to gain peace with Israel. He experienced political isolation among neighbouring countries. For this reason, he began to quiet the voices of rebellion, including religious rebellion of Islamic groups until the Israelite withdrawal from the Sinai Peninsula was complete.

FUNNY MOMENTS

Even though Bishop Beimen endured hardships and misbehaviour from the prison guards, he narrated several humorous stories to us.

• Bishop Beimen used to call out from under his door to Bishop Benyamin of Al-Monofeya, jokingly saying, "Father, all these problems are from Al-Monofeya!". President Sadat, who ordered their imprisonment, was originally from Al-Monofeya.

• Bishop Beimen and other prisoners often would try to get some air by breathing under the door. In light of this he once jokingly said, "They put our noses to the floor!"

• The prison guard used to trust Bishop Beimen so much pertaining to the prison inmates that he said to him, "I am the guard, but you are the one who gives the orders". The fathers started calling Bishop Beimen the abbot of the prison. He became known as bishop over the diocese of Malawy, Ansena, El-Ashmoneen, El-Marg, Abu Zabal and El-Kanater and all the prisons in Egypt. May the Lord preserve his life Amen! They used to joke with him that his diocese extended to accommodate for all prisons in Egypt.

• Bishop Beimen used to call the prison of El-Marg the Sheraton of El-Marg. He commented that the lentils they used to eat had cockroaches in it. The prison guard saw the cockroaches and said, "You embarrass us in front of the bishops!"

• Rats used to enter the prison cells in Leiman Wadi El-Natroun and crawled around and over the faces of Fr. Tadrous Yacoub and Fr. Louka Sidarous, which would usually awake them. One of the bishops asked them what was wrong and they replied, "There were rats crawling on our faces." The Bishop then jokingly asked, "Before they crawled on your faces, did they take absolution?"

A VISION IN CELL 23

BISHOP BEIMEN

The late Bishop Beimen truly felt in the spirit that great tribulations were about to imminently hit the Coptic Orthodox Church in Egypt. Just two days before he was imprisoned, a doctor and his wife visited Bishop Beimen and they told him that great tribulations were about to start very soon!

Orders came from Lieutenant Mohammad El-Nabawy Ismail, the minister of Internal Affairs, to imprison Bishop Beimen for 'Religious Extremism'! Lieutenant Ismail from the National Security, headed by Mr. Omar Abdel-Gawwad wanted to fabricate false accusations against him that incited religious conflict between Christians and Muslims. In one incident, a police officer went to the house of Mr. Nabil Basilius Fam, an Anglican deacon and lawyer, to try and get him to disclose personal information about Bishop Beimen. Their plans were to get him to accuse Bishop Beimen of being discriminatory towards Protestants, however, their plans failed when Mr. Nabil said to them, "He (Bishop Beimen) is a very good man". Subsequently the officers quickly excused themselves, saying that they were busy and had other matters to deal with.

On Thursday 3rd September 1981, the late Bishop Beimen was returning from a retreat in the El-Muharraq Monastery after taking confessions from a lot of the youth. When he arrived at his residence, he was given a message that the head of the police Mr. Yehya Abdel-Razzak insisted to speak with him. He called Mr. Abdel-Razzak to ask what the issue was about, while Lieutenant Mohammad Abdel-Khalek conveyed to him that he needed to see Bishop Beimen immediately to take his opinion on an urgent matter. Bishop Beimen said that his driver was unavailable to escort him to the meeting, and alternatively a police car could be arranged to transport him. Bishop Beimen apologised saying he would prefer not to travel with a police car as they are very uncomfortable due to his deteriorating health. He then asked the late Mr. Helmy Shafik Basili, a famous auto-electrician, to drive him to El-Menia.

When Bishop Beimen entered the Lieutenant's office, he found that the Lieutenant was in a very bad mood and quite busy. He politely said to him: "You seem to be busy now, can I come back later?" The Lieutenant replied, "You cannot leave this place." Bishop Beimen was surprised at his response. The lieutenant asked Bishop Beimen to send for some of his clothes and medications from Mallawy, as he might be spending a couple of days in Cairo. He refused because he thought that such an action would raise alarm in Mallawy and wanted to avoid raising any concerns with the police in Mallawy as they had a good relationship. Bishop Beimen was loved by all Christians and Muslims in Mallawy. The Lieutenant expressed though, that there was a serious problem between the church and the country and that he might be able to help resolve the issue.

The Lieutenant saw that in such circumstances and to follow protocol, the police required the accused person to be escorted in their (Jeep) car to the intended place. Bishop Beimen refused to travel in a Jeep as it might cause his stitches to rip open, all at the fault of the police. Thus, the police allowed him to use his own personal car to travel back to Cairo while being escorted by a uniformed officer.

When Bishop Beimen arrived in Giza, the accompanying uniformed officer was called back to his station and told to inform Bishop Beimen that he would be transported to El-Marg prison. The officer was disappointed about the news but obligated to inform Bishop Beimen that National Security required that he be taken into custody at El-Marg prison.

At El-Matareya, Bishop Beimen bought the newspaper on Friday 4th of September, which was against protocol for a person being transported to prison. He saw an article on the first page that read, "Imprisonment of Christian and Muslim religious leaders, and allocating them in safe places until further investigations, continue today." What was astonishing was that President Sadat thought that prisons were a safe place to put these religious leaders! Bishop Beimen gently said to the accompanying officer, "I think I might be part of the people about to be imprisoned". The officer smiled at him and nodded 'Yes', then he confiscated the newspaper from him. Bishop

Beimen then knew that he was being led to El-Marg prison and began to mentally prepare himself.

Originally El-Marg prison was a palace for one of the former reigning princes. It was the same place used to imprison the people of the revolution in July 1952 against the first President of the Arab Republic of Egypt, President Mohammad Naguib.

FIRST IMPRESSIONS ABOUT THE EL-MARG PRISON:

When Bishop Beimen arrived with the accompanying officer of El-Marg prison on the morning of Friday 4th September, he met an officer from National Security who aggressively commented on the fact that he had come in his own private Mercedes car to prison. He searched his bag thoroughly and was outraged when he found a little bottle of oil used for church sacraments that he thought was a bottle of perfume. He also wanted to strip search Bishop Beimen, as he previously did to other priests and laymen.

While Bishop Beimen was being interrogated, Mr. Mahmoud El-Gameel arrived. He saw the face of the officer accompanying him and noticed that he was crying. The accompanying officer said to him, "This is a beloved man, why are you treating him like this? He does not deserve this!" The prison officer exempted Bishop Beimen from being strip searched and instead directed that he be sent directly to his cell. When Bishop Beimen started to walk towards his cell he was called back by the officer. The officer said to him, "This could all possibly be a huge mistake that we are trying to rectify." This sparked some hope in Bishop Beimen who thought that he might be soon released from prison. Unfortunately, though, he was only called back in order that the accompanying officer who was saddened by his imprisonment could farewell him. The officer hugged him and cried, saying, "God willing this matter will be resolved quickly so that you can return to us again." The prison officer then led him back to his cell and loudly demanded that his name be entered into the record as 'Bishop Beimen from Mallawy'.

After all of the prison inmates heard about Bishop Beimen's imprisonment, suddenly there was an uproar from the cells where the people cried out, "Even Bishop Beimen! This is a disaster!". The number of voices calling out indicated that there were a lot of church members imprisoned, and it was becoming obvious that this was a ferocious attack against the Church.

Mr. Basili who had transported H.G. Bishop Beimen into prison returned to the diocese with the Bishop's car and the shepherd's staff that belonged to him. Emotionally, he told everybody the news of his imprisonment.

Bishop Beimen appeared to be the only person who was

imprisoned and treated politely during the interrogation process. He was loved by all people, including highly ranked officials in the police department of El-Menia, and his imprisonment led to much displeasure and disapproval. Everybody knew very well that Bishop Beimen was against religious fanaticism and demonstrated support for national unity. The imprisonment impacted the congregation of Mallawy greatly as everybody loved and adored him, both Christians and Muslims alike. The Christian congregation prayed fervently with many tears in liturgies for him.

After Bishop Beimen had been imprisoned, his brothers in the ministry met together to consider what options were available to try and release him from prison. They had often heard that Lieutenant Abdel-Wadood, the assistant to the minister of internal affairs for upper Egypt, was a close friend of Bishop Beimen and often visited the diocese in Mallawy. He said to people, "I used to love visiting this man (Bishop Beimen) and spending time talking with him". Thus, Bishop Beimen's brothers went to Lieutenant Helmy in Tahreer Square, whose office was located next to Lieutenant Hasan Abu-Basha, the first assistant to the minister of internal affairs. Lieutenant Helmy was infuriated saying, "How did this happen? I am the first assistant in Upper Egypt and I hear this news from newspapers!" Lieutenant Hasan Abu-Basha said to Bishop Beimen's brothers, "These are dire times!". Also, Lieutenant Helmy interjected saying, "We need to send him clothes and his medications. Send it with an officer, and do not get involved in this matter". The officers called the prison guards and with difficulty had the bag processed through the prison admissions. However, the chief officer of National Security seized the bag into storage and did not inform Bishop Beimen, who really was in dire need of his medications.

PRISON INMATES WITH BISHOP BEIMEN IN THE INTERROGATION ROOM

The interrogation room of the prison was the first stage of the imprisonment where the officers try to break down the prisoner's will to fight back and resist. This inhumane cell was intended only for one inmate in solitary confinement, though Bishop Beimen was accompanied by a few other inmates. The inmates present were:

(a) Bishop Wissa of El-Balina and affiliated regions of Berdise, Awlad El-Towk East. He was ordained a Bishop on the same day as Bishop Beimen on 22nd June 1975. Due to Bishop Beimen being older than Bishop Wissa, he allowed Bishop Beimen to sleep on a mattress that was 10 cm thick, while he slept on the floor with his coat.

(b) A left-winged university professor who was a Christian.

(c) A left-winged journalist who was also a Christian.

GOD DEALS WITH BISHOP BEIMEN THROUGH VISIONS

Bishop Beimen spent the first two days of his imprisonment in a very saddened state, almost to the point of despair. He asked God, "why was he in prison and what had he done to deserve this"? There were no political issues in Mallawy! All of Egypt could defend him as the one person that worked towards removing any misunderstandings between National Security forces and the surrounding dioceses. It was a complete and utter shock to his brothers to find out that he had been imprisoned and they wept at this injustice. Bishop Beimen was also very upset but he found strength in serving God and in the Bible, such as the verse, "Call upon Me in the day of trouble; I will deliver you, and you shall glorify Me" (Ps 50: 15).

Bishop Beimen once stood up praying fervently and saw a vision. In the vision, he was in a church giving a sermon to about 3000 people attending on a Sunday night. Suddenly, a black and evil hand came into the church and threw two or three explosive devices that caused the death of about 40 to 50 people. Bishop Beimen was very troubled by the explosion and asked, "Who did this?". He heard a voice speaking to him and saying, "Which is better, for you to be in prison or for this to happen?" Bishop Beimen then understood from this vision that God was saving Mallawy by allowing him to be imprisoned, rather than allowing a confrontation between Muslims and Christians to occur. Indeed, Bishop Beimen later disclosed that the Islamic extremists began to focus on the state of the nation, rather than the church. Furthermore, the same extremists who had previously troubled the church were the ones that protected the diocese against military attacks. They warned that whoever dared to come near the diocese would not return to their families. Bishop Beimen thanked God for this vision and his spirit was uplifted again. He started to preach to his fellow inmates, through holes in the prison walls, saying, "My beloved, if God had not allowed the imprisonments to occur, they would not have occurred. Thus, be sure that it's God's will that we are in here now and that all things are working together for good and the safety of our church and nation. Do not be worried."

The orders for the imprisonment of all clergy and laity were announced on Saturday night, the 5th September 1981 in front of the People's Assembly and the Senate.

SUFFERING INSIDE THE PRISON

Dr. Milad Hanna wrote a very descriptive account of what occurred inside the prison in his book, "Monks behind bars". Below is part of his account;

During the first few days, we were not allowed to eat and food was not allowed from outside the prison. There were no lights inside. We did not own anything except what we had on our backs. Our clothes became very dirty and smelly, and we began to complain until they gave us some new underwear.

The prison cells were originally designed for a sole prisoner in solitary confinement, measuring 2 m by 1.5 m and a height of 2 m. There was a hole in the ground, which was beyond disgusting, that was supposed to be used as the toilet. In addition, there was a tap on top of this hole.

Fr. Athanasius Boutros Soliman and Fr. Abdel-Maseeh Abu El-Kheer said, "The toilet in their cell was separated from the rest of the cell by a very low wall. Using the toilet became a very embarrassing ordeal every time. The door of the cell was made of solid metal, with a small window about 10 cm x 10 cm at a height of about 160 cm. This was the only source of fresh air into the cell. Some prisoners used to breathe in air from the bottom slit of the door. Other fathers used towels to move the air around to try and spread fresh air into the cell.

Dr. Milad Hanna continues his account, "It was getting more crowded in the cells every day, to the extent that the cell which was built for one prisoner would accommodate three inmates! Sleeping in these cells became nearly impossible. Every time you wanted to turn around, you had to excuse yourself and apologise for the trouble you would cause to the other inmates. This situation reminded me of chicken pieces on a skewer!

The smell of sweat, body odour and the foul stench of the toilet became too overwhelmingly nauseating. The cracks in the walls were entry points for cockroaches and unnamed insects. The unmistakable and troubling noise of mosquitoes at night became a cause of many nightmares, and their bites were unsettling. I asked the prison officer "why are there so many mosquitoes around"? His answer was that the prison was near a sewerage system that travelled towards the yellow mountain, which seemed believable.

A tin that would usually be used to collect rubbish from the streets was used to distribute food to the inmates. Another prisoner who worked in the kitchen used his dirty hands to offer a small piece of white cheese to eat with our bread. Despite these appalling practices, since we were starving, we were willing to eat whatever was given to us and were even thankful.

We became accustomed to being hungry and living in darkness in the prison cell. The darkness carried some nasty surprises, such as the fact that the beans contained dead insects and the white cheese contained live worms! The prison guards left every day at 4 p.m., leaving police officers and just one police guard inside the guard's room.

Bishop Beimen recalls that, "The cell was very narrow, and the toilet flush usually drained into the room where we slept. We were only allowed half an hour outside the cell each day. Sometimes the drain would be blocked and the contents would seep out into the mattresses that we slept on. The food was infested with dead insects and cockroaches, and possibly other things. In terms of my medications, I was given only one tablet even though I was required to take three tablets daily. When I asked for the other medications, I would have to wait hours before receiving them. Another prison inmate was usually allowed to leave his cell and walk around to buy food outside, and his family could visit too. He could bring his own clothes into the prison. However, among the clergy imprisoned, initially we weren't allowed any of these luxuries."

Bishop Beimen once asked the prison guards if he could eat some honey, especially since the quality of the food served in prison was quite poor. The prison guards refused to give him honey because it was only served in glass containers, and according to prison protocol, inmates are not allowed access to glass in case of using it as a weapon for violence or self-harm. Later though, the guards provided honey to Bishop Beimen in plastic containers. Without a doubt the lack of proper food and adequate medication led to the deterioration of Bishop

Beimen's health.

Bishop Wissa often spoke about Bishop Beimen, his prison cellmate. He told us that Bishop Beimen used to wear prescription glasses all day and take them off before sleep. He suffered severely poor eyesight due to a condition called liver cirrhosis. Bishop Beimen was highly sensitive to his surroundings, making it difficult to sleep. For example, if a person in the cell was snoring, he would really struggle to sleep. He also suffered painful physical problems when there was high humidity in the cell. His fever spiked a few times while in prison but was careful not to show any signs of discomfort.

Dr. Mohammad Zaki Sweedan, the physician who treated Bishop Beimen, was surprised to see him alive after being imprisoned. In fact, Dr. Sweedan went to visit Bishop Beimen and began crying saying, "I did not think that you would come out of prison alive with your medical condition. I lost all hope and thought that you would have had internal bleeding and pass away in prison." Indeed, it has been written, "The right hand of the Lord does valiantly. The right hand of the Lord is exalted; The right hand of the Lord does valiantly. I shall not die, but live, and declare the works of the Lord." (Psalm 118: 15-17). A rumour spread that Bishop Beimen had passed away in prison, which led to the diocese representative, Mr. Gerges Abdel-Maseeh, frequently visiting the prison to make sure that Bishop Beimen was alive and well.

Bishop Beimen recounts the story of a time when a man with an internal position in prison said to him, "Bishop Beimen you can rest assured now, they will take you to hospital to receive medical attention under the supervision of Dr. Rashad El-Rouby". However, Bishop Beimen insisted on staying, saying, "I have other doctors and specialists that know my condition and I can't just change them now." After his release from prison, Bishop Beimen travelled to London to visit gastroenterologist Prof. Sheila Sherlock. When Prof. Sherlock checked on him, she told him that his liver condition advanced in degeneration about 10 years. She was quoted saying amidst his deteriorating liver, "However, thank God that He got you out, and supported you during your imprisonment". Bishop Beimen was very happy to hear these words from a non-religious person. This professor later visited him in his sister's house a few months before his departure, while she attended a conference about liver diseases nearby.

EL-MARG PRISON TURNS INTO A MONASTERY

Fr Athanasius Boutros explains how E-Marg prison effectively became a monastery, and the prison cells effectively became monastic cells:

"On the first day of my imprisonment I heard a loud voice saying, "My brothers, listen to me please. My name is Samir Tadrous and I'm a journalist from the newspaper El-Ahram. I'm used to prison life and I want to present you, my experience. We will conduct announcements about every new prisoner and why he has been imprisoned. Thus, please stand and come close to your cell door to introduce yourself, starting from the cell closest to the main prison door." Within half an hour we had been introduced to seven bishops, twenty-four priests and twenty-four laymen.

Mr. Samir Tadrous had been imprisoned according to the decree to imprison any 'trouble-making' journalists from any newspaper publishers. This was introduced when President El-Sadat asked all newspaper publishers to remove these 'trouble-maker' journalists, as seen with the imprisonment of many Christians in September 1981.

The next morning when Mr. Samir Tadrous began the announcements, Bishop Beimen spoke up saying, "We thank you Mr. Tadrous for your experience that you shared with us. You know that we are religious men and would like to spend our lives as deemed fit. We will divide the days of the week so that each bishop can lead us in daily prayer. We will have morning prayers, hourly prayers, bible studies and spiritual talks, followed by sunset prayers and midnight praises."

Through the small window in his cell, Bishop Beimen consecutively gave sermons for 40 days lasting about two hours every evening after sunset prayers. Despite being very sick and in need of constant medical attention due to his many illnesses, he did not cease to teach from the bible. He gave commentaries on six of the epistles of St. Paul, focusing mainly on the epistles he wrote in imprisonment. He also took a lot of time to deeply contemplate and explain the book of Hebrews. After the sermons, Bishop Beimen took some questions from the prisoners without being able to see their faces. A person would speak up and say, "Can I ask you a question, Your Grace?". Bishop Beimen would answer saying, "Yes, but who's asking?" The person would respond saying, "I am Father 'such and such' from prison cell 'such and such'." Bishop Beimen would typically respond saying, "Go ahead, father".

It must be mentioned that none of the prison guards ever intervened or stopped the prayers inside prison. Indeed, Bishop Beimen had carried on his shoulders the responsibility of teaching and guiding others in El-Marg prison. He continued this practice until he was released with the first group on the 12th of January 1982.

Dr. Milad Hanna said, "Bishop Beimen experienced the longest imprisonment among the clergy, and was acting as an intermediary between the inmates and prison guards. He was naturally a leader and his teaching ability was reflected through in great and thorough knowledge of the bible. Despite his many illnesses, he was the most active of all the other inmates."

THE CASE SURROUNDING BISHOP BEIMEN

The criminal case of Bishop Beimen began at Lazoghli Square on Tuesday 24th of November 1981, on the feast day of St. Mina the miracle performer. Mr. Shaker El-Gebali, a muslim lawyer, volunteered to represent Bishop Beimen. Mr. Shaker had previously been imprisoned, accused of abetting the Islamic extremists on two occasions, both after the revolution and another time in 1968. Mr. Shaker was imprisoned both times for one year in duration. The other lawyer that represented Bishop Beimen was Mr. Edward Marcus Bishay, the diocese attorney.

Mr. Bishay began preparing the papers as evidence of Bishop Beimen's innocence. The day before Mr. Bishay was scheduled to travel, Mr. Shaker asked to accompany him to help assist him in representing Bishop Beimen. Mr. Bishay agreed and they both travelled together the next morning. Initially the case was postponed for two days and they had to travel back to Mallawy due to their working commitments. After returning to the prosecutor's office for the second time they found that the case was postponed again. On the third journey, they went into the office of investigations in Lazoghli Square, Cairo, for a third time and the case file was incredibly postponed once more.

Anybody that was detained for questioning in the prosecutor's office could only spend five minutes with his family, even if the family travelled very far away! During the investigation, those detained would go in for questioning one at a time. Through God's grace the investigator was a police officer based in Mallawy for three years and he recognised Mr. Shaker. When Bishop Beimen arrived for questioning, Mr. Shaker realised that he looked very tired and said to him, "Three times we came to be questioned, and they have sent us home. I insist that this time the questioning process of the investigation goes ahead."

THE QUESTIONING

When the assistant investigator arrived, he fired his first accusation towards Bishop Beimen saying, "You are accused of being a religious extremist." Bishop Beimen began to cry at the implication and unfairness of such an accusation, especially as he spent his entire life dedicated towards national unity. Mr. Bishay came forth to defend Bishop Beimen saying, "Sir, we can accept any accusation against Bishop Beimen, except for religious extremism." Mr. Shaker also came forth saying, "I am a Muslim lawyer, and what I am saying is true in front of God. Bishop Beimen assists twenty Muslim families in this area." Then he asked Mr. Bishay to bring out all supporting evidence.

The assistant investigator was astonished at the evidence presented. He began to calm Bishop Beimen down saying, "I know you're a good man, father, and God willing this will be over and nothing will happen." Bishop Beimen's brothers also left a few of his books that promoted national unity, forgiveness, love, and acceptance. The investigator was more than astonished and began to record all of this as evidence for his innocence. After he viewed Bishop Beimen's publications, he was very respectful towards him. Most of the remaining questions were not about the case anymore, but rather the conflict that arose between Pope Shenouda III and President El-Sadat.

One of the accusations against Bishop Beimen was that he met with doctors and pharmacists at the beginning of his bishopric in Mallawy. Subsequently the assistant investigator asked sarcastically, "Why didn't you mention garbage collectors also? What do you need from educated people?". Another accusation was that Bishop Beimen met with religious teachers. Bishop Beimen responded saying that he oversaw implementing the religious curriculum in the department of education, and these teachers assisted him. The assistant investigator commented sarcastically, "You should have included the Sheiks in implementing this curriculum."

After a relatively amicable ending to their conversation, the assistant investigator admitted that Bishop Beimen was a lighthearted man. By the end of the investigation, he said to Bishop Beimen, "Relax, after this investigation is over, I will come and visit you in Mallawy." He then informed Bishop Beimen that his brothers were outside and that they could come in and see him. This was against protocol, but nevertheless the investigator allowed it to happen. It's also against protocol for the defendant to find out the verdict prior to the conclusion of the investigation, however at the end of the questioning process the investigator wrote on Bishop Beimen's file 'Not guilty at all.'

Bishop Benyamin of Al-Monofeya and Bishop Bemwa, abbot of the monastery of St. George in El-Rezkiat in Luxur, also had to travel from Wadi El-Natroun prison to the office of investigations in Lazoghli Square in Cairo in the winter of 1981. This trip took them a whole day each time.

A UNIQUE RELATIONSHIP WITH THE PRISON GUARD

After Bishop Beimen was declared innocent after being questioned, he was allowed to receive visitors in prison. One night, many church members of Bishop Beimen's diocese in Mallawy came to see him. Other visitors included police officers from Mallawy, Sheiks and other non-Christians. The prison guard was astonished and asked, "What brought you all here?" They replied, "He is our father and is very important to us. We came to tell him that everybody in Mallawy misses him." The prison guard began to respect Bishop Beimen. Once a group of political figures[6] came and told the prison guard Mr. Mahmoud El-Gameel, "Just as Bishop Beimen is a bishop to the Christians, he is also a bishop to the Muslims." Mr. Mahmoud then asked Bishop Beimen, "If all those people love and respect you, why did they imprison you in the first place?!". Even Sheik Abdel-Hady went so far as to say to the prison guard that, "Bishop Beimen is my partner in the apostolic ministry!" Bishop Beimen laughed much due to their kind love and support.

Bishop Beimen described that the prison guard Mr. Mahmoud El-Gameel was a good man. He used to care for Bishop Beimen due to his medical conditions and would call and invite him infrequently to have rest in his room rather than his own cell. During that time, Bishop Beimen's brother called him through the prison guard's own personal phone line and they spoke for extended periods of time about various issues. Bishop Beimen would sometimes leave the prison guard's room after 1 a.m. after spending such a long time on the phone with his brother.

Mr. Tadrous Abdallah Saeed Attia, who was a partner in the service with Bishop Beimen in St. Mina Church in Shobra since 1950, recounted, "I remember once when Bishop Beimen was in prison with some bishops and priests in the prison of El-

6 Sheik Abdel-Hady Abdel-Salam Ahmad, Sheik Amer Shamroukh of the mosque of El-Erfany in Mallawy, Sheik Hesein Ashiry Mohammad a member of the People's Assembly in Mallawy, Mr. Sayed Ahmad Shahhat a lawyer and member of the local People's Assembly, and Mr. Abdel-Hady Ashiry Mohammad of the national assembly in Mallawy

Marg. I visited him with some brothers and Fr. Mina Ibrahim accompanied us. We came to the prison guard office and asked to see Bishop Beimen. We found Bishop Wissa of El-Balina in the room with the prison guard, and he leaned in and whispered to me, 'Ask for any other person except for Bishop Beimen because you will find Bishop Beimen wandering around without any guards monitoring him, and soon you will find him in this office without being summoned'. Indeed, a few minutes later, Bishop Beimen showed up in the room and we met with him. I also found out that the prison guard's son was suffering with a severe disability. Bishop Beimen had convinced the prison guard that he could help his son, and thus he agreed to bring his son to meet him. Amazingly, the physical state of the disabled child began to improve dramatically after meeting Bishop Beimen. Truly, the prison guard discovered that Bishop Beimen was a blessed man and he held him in high regard following this miracle". Mr. Tadrous also adds that when he asked the prison guard what the difference was between the bishops and priests to other prisoner inmates, his response was, "the difference between light and darkness!"

Bishop Beimen was the only person whose voice could be heard in prison, largely due to his close relationship with the prison guard and strong influence. The prison guard used to tell Bishop Beimen, "I may be the guard, but you are the one who gives the orders. Since I'm the guard and unhappy about the decision made to imprison you, I cannot be held responsible for any problems." For this reason, he used to be compassionate towards the innocent priests and bishops.

On the morning of Wednesday 7th of October 1981, the prison guard accompanied Bishop Beimen, Fr. Yousif Assad and Fr. Athanasius Boutros into the prison courtyard. The guard broke the news to them that President El-Sadat had been assassinated and when the news reached Torra prison, the inmates set fire to the blankets and mattresses. The prison guard asked Bishop Beimen, "What do you think will happen here?". Bishop Beimen replied, "I trust all the inmates in this prison. Their youngest priest oversees forty or fifty thousand people in his congregation; thus, they are very responsible men." After hearing Bishop Beimen's response, the prison guard went back inside and announced in a loud voice, "Open all the cell doors! It has been confirmed that President El-Sadat is now dead. This is an emergency!"

The prison guard's wife was a doctor and she used to work with other Christian doctors who warned her to tell her husband to treat the Christian inmates with the respect and dignity they deserve. In fact, she said to her husband, "Watch out Mahmoud, you have to treat those Christians properly, otherwise they might pray for harm towards our kids, as they did with El-Sadat, and you know how he ended up!". Mahmoud would go into the prison cells and asked the priests and bishops, "Does anybody have any complaints about how I treat any of you?! Maybe I have upset someone with something I said or how I have treated somebody? My wife persistently warns me every night saying, 'Beware of those Christians!'". Finally, to ease the prison guard's mind he brought his two sons into prison and asked the bishops and priests to pray over them. He also brought some water that they could pray over and he took the water as a blessing home with him.

Fr. Boules Basili said, "We used to end our morning prayers with four hundred prostrations and with one voice say Lord have mercy (Keyrie Leyson). Our voices were in total harmony and would rise up from the heart, shaking the walls of the prison". The prison guard once hurriedly came and asked us, "What are you saying? What is this 'sound' that you keep on repeating?". We explained to him the meaning of the words Keyrie Leyson. He said to us, "Okay, but please be gentle when you say it otherwise the prison walls might actually collapse and fall down on us". After a while the prison guard confessed to the fathers that his behaviour had significantly changed. He said, "I used to swear, get angry, and use violence, which is common practice among prison guards. Now though, you've made me forget all those bad habits due to your good behaviour. I can no longer be a prison guard". We later found out that he took unpaid leave and started a business.

The relationship between Bishop Beimen and the prison guard Mr. Mahmoud El-Gameel over the short period that Bishop Beimen spent in prison, between 3rd of September 1981 to 13th of January 1982, continued to grow stronger after he was released from prison. Remarkably, Mr. Mahmoud came and visited Bishop Beimen in his sister's apartment in Shobra to take his blessings.

THE FEAST AND THE ALTAR

With the feast of the Nativity approaching, the fathers wanted to pray and celebrate the liturgy for this major feast, and Bishop Beimen asked the prison guard if they could do so in prison. The guard responded, "I do not think the National Security will allow you to do so." Bishop Beimen went on to explain that this liturgy will appease all the fathers and the prison guards can monitor us the entire time from the surveillance room. The prison guard called National Security for permission and they responded, "There is no harm in letting them pray a liturgy."

The priests and bishops imprisoned at El-Marg asked for a holy board and holy utensils, along with the liturgical garments in order to pray the liturgy. Bishop Paula of Tanta delivered the holy bread for the liturgy and the fathers used one of the prison guard's desk as an altar after placing the holy board over it with bed covers. The fathers also made a simple icon for the nativity.

The setting for the liturgy was a beautiful layout, much like the Catacombs in Rome when the early Christians prayed liturgies under persecution. In total eight bishops, twenty-four priests and about 120 of the laity prayed the Nativity liturgy, along with about 30 other inmates. Later, after the feast of Epiphany, empty fruit baskets were alternatively used as an altar when we were no longer allowed to use the prison officer's desk.

Fr. Athanasius Boutros[7] explains that the prison was made up of two wards enclosed in the same building; one ward for the laity and the other for the priests and bishops. Both doors to each prison ward were opened throughout the liturgical prayer, while a place was prepared in the corner of the ward for the laity where the altar was set up. The main entrance to the prison was shut as usual.

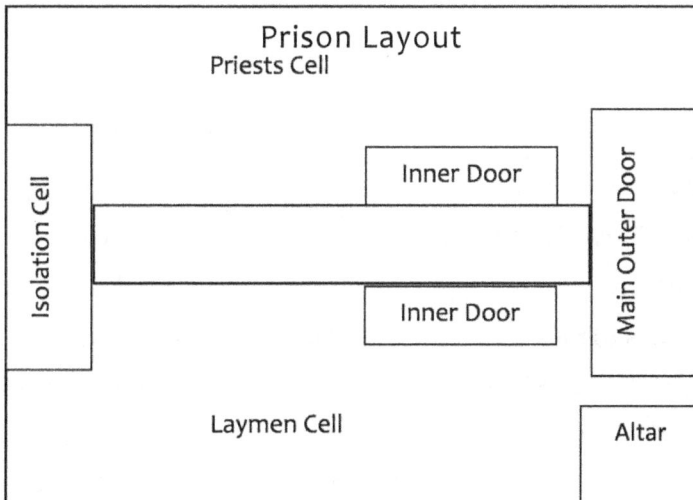

Prison Layout

Priests Cell

Isolation Cell	Inner Door	Main Outer Door
	Inner Door	
Laymen Cell		Altar

7 Fr Athanasius Boutros was a priest in the Church of Archangel Michael and St George in El-Matareya

CONTEMPLATIONS OF BISHOP BEIMEN ON
THE PRISON EXPERIENCE

a) Even though the fathers were imprisoned with inmates who had contagious diseases, they never contracted any of these diseases, nor even a snake bite, heart attack or stroke. The Lord guarded and defended them, "Behold, He who keeps Israel Shall neither slumber nor sleep. The Lord is your keeper." (Psalm 121: 4-5)

b) Being a bishop is not about wearing different clothes, or a different head cover, nor is it wearing glamorous garments, or about people kissing your hands and giving you plenty of respect. It's about being humble, carrying the cross and serving at others.

c) Our orthodox faith is not through words, for many have given sermons that influenced others, but the true depth of Christianity is carrying the cross, just like the fathers joyfully and thankfully carried their cross in El-Marg prison and Leiman Wadi El-Natroun. "If anyone desires to come after Me, let him deny himself, and take up his cross, and follow Me" (Matthew 16: 24). The spirituality of orthodoxy is by action, not merely words.

d) Pain can be endured in the company of others. The fathers that were imprisoned in the prison of El-Marg and Leiman Wadi

El-Natroun loved each other as one. Just as the early Christians lived with one spirit and heart, to the extent that they did not keep any money for themselves, but proclaimed "the multitude of those who believed were of one heart and one soul; neither did anyone say that any of the things he possessed was his own, but they had all things in common." (Acts 4: 32)

THE RELEASE OF BISHOP BEIMEN

On Tuesday 12th of January 1982 an announcement was made that Bishop Beimen would be released from prison. This news was announced at St. Mark's Church in Malawy directly before the engagement prayer of Salah El-Deen Adib Marcus Bishay.[8] Fr. Yousif Khalil Ayoub announced the news before the engagement.

Bishop Beimen was released on Wednesday 13th of January, along with Bishop Fam of Tamma, Fr. Yousif Assad of St Mary's Church in El-Omraneya, El-Giza and Fr. Bishoy Yassa.

Bishop Beimen was released following an important meeting on Tuesday 12th of January 1982 with Lieutenant Hassan Abu Basha, the minister of internal affairs in the new government reign of President Hosny Mubarak. He accompanied the other

8 Salah El-Deen Adib Marcus Bishay was, ironically, the brother of Mr. Edward Marcus, the diocese lawyer

fathers who were released to the Lieutenant's office. Bishop Beimen made a good impression on Lieutenant Hassan who said, "You were wrongly imprisoned and I'm certain of your commitment and efforts towards nationalism." He added, "If you want, you can leave the prison tonight. Collect your things and go." Bishop Beimen replied, "I would rather leave tomorrow and take my time." Thus, the next morning, Wednesday 13th of January 1982, Bishop Beimen farewelled the prison guards and officers, but just as he was about to leave, Lieutenant Hassan Abu Basha said to Bishop Beimen, "Please do not go back to Mallawy right now because the security is quite bad and I won't be able to ensure your safety at the moment. Wait until things have settled down, then you can go back." Thus, Bishop Beimen complied to stay.

AN INTERVIEW WITH BISHOP BEIMEN FOR THE MAGAZINE "AL-MOSAWWER", AFTER HIS RELEASE

On Tuesday 12th of January 1982 an announcement was made that Bishop Beimen would be released from prison. This news was announced at St. Mark's Church in Malawy directly before the engagement prayer of Salah El-Deen Adib Marcus Bishay. Fr. Yousif Khalil Ayoub announced the news before the engagement.

Bishop Beimen was released on Wednesday 13th of January,

along with Bishop Fam of Tamma, Fr. Yousif Assad of St Mary's Church in El-Omraneya, El-Giza and Fr. Bishoy Yassa.

Bishop Beimen was released following an important meeting on Tuesday 12th of January 1982 with Lieutenant Hassan Abu Basha, the minister of internal affairs in the new government reign of President Hosny Mubarak. He accompanied the other fathers who were released to the Lieutenant's office. Bishop Beimen made a good impression on Lieutenant Hassan who said, "You were wrongly imprisoned and I'm certain of your commitment and efforts towards nationalism." He added, "If you want, you can leave the prison tonight. Collect your things and go." Bishop Beimen replied, "I would rather leave tomorrow and take my time." Thus, the next morning, Wednesday 13th of January 1982, Bishop Beimen farewelled the prison guards and officers, but just as he was about to leave, Lieutenant Hassan Abu Basha said to Bishop Beimen, "Please do not go back to Mallawy right now because the security is quite bad and I won't be able to ensure your safety at the moment. Wait until things have settled down, then you can go back." Thus, Bishop Beimen complied to stay.

BISHOP BEIMEN DENIED ENTRY TO MALLAWY

Bishop Beimen was denied entry to Mallawy after he was released Wednesday 13th January 1982, due to safety concerns. Bishop Beimen chose then to travel to other residences for his safety; including his older brother's house in Masr El-Gedida, his younger brother's house in El-Mohandessin, his sister's house in Shobra and often to El-Muharraq monastery. Bishop Beimen was still able to be connected with his diocese via the phone. He also appointed his brother, the beloved Bishop Arsanius of El-Menia and Abu Korkas, to run the management of the diocese on his behalf during his absence.

BISHOP BEIMEN'S DELAYED ARRIVAL TO HIS DIOCESE

It is worth mentioning that Bishop Beimen's release from prison was attributed to the love from the members of the People's Assembly who sought his return before their elections in 1985 in light of Bishop Beimen's deteriorating health. The members were concerned that Bishop Beimen might pass away before returning to his diocese, which potentially could have been very contentious among Christians.

Fr. Marcus Salama Rophail and Fr. Boutros Gayed Saeed started a petition for the return of Bishop Beimen to his diocese and Mr. Hesein Ashiri Mohammad (a member of the People's Assembly in the National Party in Mallawy) presented this petition to the governor of El-Menia, Mr. Salah El-Deen Ibrahim, after receiving approval from the minister of internal affairs Mr. Hasan Abu Basha and prime minister Foad Mohey El-Deen.

Bishop Beimen returned to his diocese late in the night on Saturday 12th of May 1984, about two years and four months after his release from prison. As a safety precaution, his return was without any major celebration; for example, there was no ringing of bells that usually marks the return of a bishop to his diocese. He prayed his first Holy Liturgy, along with Fr. Mina Matta Abdel Maseeh, after returning back on Sunday 13th of May 1984. Once the people discovered that Bishop Beimen had returned many people came to see him. In fact, more than ten thousand people came to congratulate him on his safe return to his diocese, and Bishop Beimen greeted each person individually. Everybody wanted to hug and kiss him after seeing him back home. In fact, after exerting such great effort greeting the people in the church Bishop Beimen fainted from exhaustion. It is important to note that Bishop Beimen was sick several times in prison and after having experienced internal bleeding on multiple occasions, he always wore black garments when sleeping to prevent anybody noticing and panicking seeing any internal bleeding. He was always concerned about his congregation treating him with too much praise or unnecessary concern.

Mr. Adel Awny Sherta, secretary of Bishop Beimen, said, "After his imprisonment, Bishop Beimen began to treat people of high authority differently as he sensed that they wrote conflicting reports about him." Despite being ill-treated, Bishop Beimen always treated his adversaries with love and often gave them gifts, yet they stubbornly continued to attack him. I remember once when the director of the State Security Investigation, Mr. Omar Abdel Gawad, came to visit Bishop Beimen. Bishop Beimen told me to ask him first whether this visit was official or just a personal visit. After I asked him, he replied that he only wanted to greet the bishop. Bishop Beimen came down and I was surprised that he hugged and kissed Mr. Abdel Gawad on his forehead. When Mr. Abdel Gawad departed, I asked Bishop Beimen why he treated him differently. Bishop Beimen replied, "because I placed the blame on him when he wrote a report against me during my imprisonment."

A STORY ON THE SIDELINE OF IMPRISONMENT

The national security asked Mr. Hesein Ashiri Mohammad (a member of the People's Assembly in the National Party in Mallawy) to choose a local Christian association to foreclose as part of the decisions of 5th of September 1981. He chose the association called 'Salvation of Souls' in Mallawy, which wasn't a strictly religious association. Pending its foreclosure, its members filed a law suit against the decision and after two years they were permitted to reopen the association. Thankfully due to God's grace the services of this association commenced once again and grew stronger than priorly being foreclosed.

BISHOP BEIMEN'S OPINION ON THE EFFECTS OF BEING IMPRISONED FOR THE CONGREGATION IN MALLAWY

FIRST THOUGHT:

The congregation prayed fervently when they were in tribulations: through the grace of Christ, the people of Mallawy learned how to appropriately deal with tribulations. They decided to pray a Holy Liturgy and partake of communion every day. They used to recount stories of a priest who used to pray the liturgy and cry during one of the litany prayers, often struggling to finish the prayer. The congregation of Mallawy also had nightly prayer meetings, and with much supplications and prayers they made their requests known to God, the true source of peace. They learned that prayer is the only solution for our many tribulations as Christians. Truly the Lord gave us through the inner room of prayer, and the altar, the resolution to all our problems. For a long-standing this has been the experience of Christians. During the time of the apostles, they were forced to hide in secret places to raise fervent prayers. During the time of persecution, prayer was the source of strength and unity of the Church. The experience of the people of Mallawy praying fervently was not limited to this congregation alone, but for the Church as a whole. During tribulation the church does not resort to rioting or violence, or any sort of extremism, but prayer.

We have a path that Christ Himself drew for us through prayer when He said, "Ask, and it will be given to you; seek, and you will find; knock, and it will be opened to you" (Matthew 7: 7). We take this as a promise and He is faithful to give us according to His goodness. This is the first experience that collectively the congregation of Mallawy carried out, and it was truly marvellous to witness.

SECOND THOUGHT

The strong love for the bishop: there is some people who lack understanding and completely refuse to follow the bishop. However, I believe that God has entrusted me with a calling and bestowed upon me knowledge and discernment to shepherd my flock. For example, in one instance I stood firm that a girl should be at least 16 years of age before getting married and this initially caused much contention from the uneducated people of the villages who wanted their girls to be married in line with their physical maturity. There were other misconceptions among the congregation such as the existence of magic spells, but I believed in defending the truth. As an analogy I related my experience to St. John Chrysostom who could have very easily won over the Emperor and Empress if he had just conformed to them, however, I believe this is not the method of a Christian.

After being imprisoned, the attitude of the congregation began to change significantly. A lot of people only felt the importance of having a bishop in the diocese until I was imprisoned. After I was unavailable, the congregation began to value my presence and sacrifice for the diocese. I sacrificed my comfort for theirs, and they did not realise this until I was gone. Through the grace of God, I formed new organisations, more services and increased the number of servants. Truly the fruits of the service became my consolation in prison. On the day that I returned to my diocese, more than 10,000 people attended and warmly greeted me.

Today, I thank God that even if I have to travel to Europe for medical reasons, I will rest assured that the diocese will run as normal as the people know their service. The congregation knows how to maintain the unity of the church. The people in the diocese have improved their attitude and the diocese has flourished - as evidenced with 27 newly ordained priests, ten deaconesses and five consecrated deacons. Among the new organisations and services; they include a printing and visual aid committee, social services, and family and village development committees. All these organisations are active and self-sufficient. I believe that the people of the diocese are working together in harmony and unity, rather than having conflicts with one another. This is all due to the grace of God.

THIRD THOUGHT

The unity between Christians and Muslims was stronger than ever before: I expected that there would be a great division between Christians and Muslims, particularly after the imprisonment of many clergy and laity members. However, when our Muslim brothers witnessed how accepting and joyful, we were despite being imprisoned, and how much we respected our fellow Muslim leaders, the Muslims and Christians united. In fact, love began to grow even stronger between Christians and Muslims in Mallawy. When I told them stories of how the Muslim brothers treated me with love, the extremist Christians settled down and began to have positive thoughts towards their Muslim brothers. This unity is very important and hopefully will spread throughout the whole country.

FOURTH THOUGHT

The comfort that we received amid tribulation: every one of us is prone to tribulations, such as experiencing mistreatment, injustice, and experiencing harm. As long as we remain in the flesh there will always be tribulations, but what can help allow others to endure such tribulations is witnessing the tremendous endurance of others. The fact that their own bishop endured significant mistreatment from others and persevered, should renew the strength of the people to endure. The people of Mallawy saw that my health deteriorated since I became a bishop in 1976, yet I didn't lose my spiritual devoutness or love towards my diocese.

Blessed be God, to whom is due all glory in tribulation and peace, sorrow and joy, pain and comfort, and in every aspect of our lives. May His name be glorified in us, His own children, and may we be submissive to His perfect will. Let us say, "I am not worthy of the least of all the mercies and of all the truth which You have shown Your servant" (Gen 32: 10). I can remember countless miracles that occurred during my bishopric. I recall the large donations collected from generous people to rebuild the churches. I recall the multitude of people who became consecrated to God in miraculous ways. I recall the servants who became priests to serve in difficult places with joy. I recall the insurmountable joy that God bestowed upon us when there were about 150 divorce cases of people who wanted to forsake Christianity for the sake of the marital conflicts, yet this number somehow fell to less than ten cases. We pray that God may resolve all our tribulations. Glory be to You O' Lord, who has given us everlasting comfort. To You belong all glory, blessing and honour forevermore. Amen.

THE DAILY DOSE

FR YOUSSEF ASSAAD

HOW WAS GOD PREPARING MY HEART?

On the morning of 6th August 1981, the appearance of a real drop of His precious Blood on the upper right part of the Holy Body during the mass reminded me of His Blood and suffering on the cross. Thus, when the time came for me to carry my cross, I would remember the sufferings of Christ. This was just 28 days before my arrest.

On Wednesday 2nd September 1981 I remember that I was busy preparing pamphlets titled 'My Church' and lectures on 'Song of Songs'. These were ready for printing by around 9.00 p.m.

On the night of my arrest, I remember that I couldn't sleep well so I started reading the book 'The Life of Prayer'. I stopped reading at 12.45 a.m., then headed to church to attend prayers.

INCIDENT OF MY ARREST

Amal, a servant, rang me at 1.00 a.m. on Thursday 3rd September 1981 asking why I just left home. I answered that I went to church to pray…. looking back now I believe that God was preparing me for imprisonment.

I left my church office briefly and when I returned, I could hear Amal through the window screaming, "Father, the police are knocking on the door saying they want to inspect the house." I said to her trembling, "Open the door for them, I'm on my way to you now."

I moved downstairs trembling from the office until I reached the front yard of the church. I found the Fiat car which belonged to the consecrated deaconesses and speedily drove it. I felt that the angel of God protected me driving so early in the morning, where many dangerous accidents have occurred. I passed by El Giza Square until I reached Nasr El Din Mosque, where I saw two police cars. I turned on the high beams and stopped in front of Khashaba Pasha's villa.

Three officers from the State Security investigators came out of the car, one of whom visited the church frequently. They told me that I was required to go to the police department and make a statement, then I could go back home in the morning. I asked them, "Why did you detain me at 2.30 a.m.? Am I a criminal such that you detain me at night and need to inspect my house? Where is your permission to do so?". One of them answered, "You will see when you get there because other people have been detained". Then I said, "Let's pass by the Metropolitan, my superior, and inform him". A colonel and some informants came to me and said, "He will know by tomorrow". I asked him to take the car back to the parking lot where I parked the car, which was just a few steps away, but he answered harshly,

"Park it here now and come with us immediately!". I parked it next to the garage on the tunnel, then I walked to the police car. The colonel then said to me, "Come and enter, O blessed one." I was astonished at these words, but didn't say anything as I entered the police car.

Just as the car started moving, I had an idea to give the Fiat car keys to the attendant working in the garage over the tunnel, responsible for the parking lot. Then I sat next to the colonel who offered me some cigarettes, but I obviously declined. I made the sign of the cross amidst all kinds of thoughts rushing through me, such as "where are we going?".

The vehicles drove through the El Maadi/Helwan route. When the police car stopped, I found myself walking on a dusty path guarded with armed soldiers and entered Turah prison at 3.15 a.m.

I entered the building via a wooden door with four panels, and then into a room in the basement which contained a bed and table. To my surprise, the investigator strip searched me, took all my belongings and made me sign a statement. He even removed the turban from my head and searched my shoes! I thought, O' Lord, what is happening? What is this all about? Many questions rushed through my mind. Had it not been for the grace of the Lord that controlled my tongue and emotions,

I would not have been able to contain myself!

Another person came in and stayed with me in the room until I reached an iron door to a cell. The officer opened it and led me in. I asked, "Is this the place where I will be imprisoned?" The officer didn't respond and locked the door. I started looking around the cell to find three cotton mattresses on the floor without blankets, two toilets and a shower. I sat down and prayed quietly.

Twenty minutes later, Fr. Ibrahim Abdu came to the same cell with an astonished face and said, "I thought I was the only one!" He started telling me how they arrested him and searched his house, and that he waited for two hours in Shobra police station until they brought him into prison. While we were talking, the cell door opened and a person wearing his pyjamas and one sandal entered. He introduced himself as Samir Amin Tadros, a left Party journalist of 'Akhbar Al Yom'. He was very surprised to see priests and Christian clergymen in the prison. At the time of his arrest, he recounted to us that he was sleeping when he heard a knock at his residence and opened the door still wearing his pyjamas to find that the police immediately threw him into a police van. His German wife ran after him only to witness the car speedily drive off.

After some silence I prayed a long prayer for Fr. Ibrahim's wife, my wife and also the whole congregation. Both Fr. Ibrahim Abdu and Samir Tadros slept for a little bit while I heard others coming into the cell next door. Samir called to them and found out that it was Bolous, an Adventist whom he knew. I heard one of the officers say, "Fr. Sarabamoun Abdu".

At 5.20 a.m. the officers called for me, opened the cell and gave me all my belongings. I knew that I was going to be transferred to another place, though I expected it to be the prosecutor's office as the officers had previously mentioned. The same car with the colonel took me to 'El-Marg Prison' at around 6.20 a.m. on Thursday 3rd September 1981. The colonel got out of the car first, then a private detective led me into the sheriff's room. I still didn't understand what was happening at the time.

IN 'EL MARG PRISON'

I arrived at El-Marg Prison at 6.50 a.m. Amidst my great astonishment, the officers took all my belongings, even the watch that I was wearing because it had a metal chain. Perhaps the guards consider the metal chain as a possible weapon. The guards only let me keep a New Testament bible and my medication.

A person from the general head of prison department and the inspector of the prison department came to transfer me. An officer holding a wireless device and a detective firmly held me until I passed through the prison's courtyard to a place called 'The Trial Prison'.

I was handed over to another detective, whom I had witnessed treating other people harshly. I prayed, "Lord please forgive him and me". I was imprisoned in cell number 16, all alone in a cell which had a small bathroom, toilet and a low tap next to it. Half an hour later, Fr. Ibrahim Abdu, whom I met in Turah Prison, entered the same cell with Mr. Bolous Fahmy. This was the beginning of our strange routine in prison. Each day, the cell door opened and the guards threw nine loaves of bread, which they call 'daily dose'. They also threw a plastic plate with maple syrup and a plate of rice with three pieces of meat. I did not even receive one serviette, towel, or a gown. I used to lie down and sit for an extended period of time without changing my attire.

With three people in such a small cell, breathing alone was a cross which required patience and tolerance. The days between Thursday 3rd September and Tuesday 8th September were a great struggle. There was no soap or even access to water, as the tap didn't work. The guards gave us some water to drink in a bucket and some more in an old tank of car oil, but when I put my hand in the bucket, I found residue oil! We were not going to drink this water!

I prayed fervently weeping, especially for Asaad my son who was unwell. When I was arrested, I was only truly comforted by his recovery through the Lord's promise, "I am the Lord your Healer". I worried a lot about my wife Amal. I wondered what had happened to her emotional state? Did the police search the house? What happened to the consecrated deaconesses, and have they been interrogated to disclose confidential information? Every time my heart increased with anxiety, I opened the New Testament and found divine words as if they were a special message to combat my great agony. I'm incapable of expressing the depth and directness of these very comforting words. Yes, I was struggling a lot, but the joy of His word truly delights our hearts.

On 8th September I was transferred to cell number 22. While they were trying to offer us better conditions by reducing the prisoners in a cell to just two people, I told them, "We're happy together." Another colonel from the prison department said to me, "You are saying no to us while we are trying to relieve you." In cell number 22, my cellmate was a youth from the church of Hadayeq El Qoba called Atallah, who worked as a mechanic. The air circulation was much better in this cell.

On 9th September, Shafiq Iskander, a 76-year-old pharmacist from Naga Hammadi was added to our cell. Clustering three people once again in the cells made breathing was difficult. My role with Mr. Iskander was to calm him down and ease his anxiety. We prayed and read daily from the Bible. Fr. Athanasius read out loud from the New Testament because no other prisoners possessed a copy except myself and him. Fr. Athanasius reading the New Testament out loud was particularly beneficial to the new prisoners.

A few days later 35 youth were transferred to Abu Zaabal Prison, along with the Bishop of Tema, eight priests and some laymen. The guards placed myself in cell number 7 with Fr. Athanasius Botrous. Each prison cell contained two people until 16th November 1981.

These were the instructions of the daily routine in the Trial Prison:

(1) The recess on our first week was 15 minutes in duration each day in the yard and later extended to 30 minutes until our release. The rest of the day was spent inside the cells. No communication was allowed with the other inmates during this time, but fortunately towards the end of our imprisonment three cells would have recess simultaneously. I thought, "O' my Lord, how bitter this is? However, I thank You for You have chosen me to carry Your cross." The cross of the Lord overshadowed the difficulties of prison life, as the image of the cross is always renewing to man. I spent most of the hours in my cell reading

the Holy Bible. I read first and second Chronicles, Ezra, Esther, Job, Psalms, Proverbs, Ecclesiastes, Song of Songs, Isaiah, Jeremiah, Lamentations, and parts of Ezekiel, while praying with tears, listening to spiritual sermons and the Holy Liturgy as comfort. Up until the 5th December 1981, I cannot forget the gift of tears as a spiritual comfort from the hand of our good Saviour.

(2) Since food from outside the prison was forbidden, eating in the prison generally took the following regime:

Breakfast: molasses with a piece of cheese, which was very salty and needed to be soaked in water for a couple of days to become edible. Sometimes the cheese had weevils and was inedible.

Lunch: served at 12 p.m. included three loaves of bread given to each one of us for the day. On Thursday, Friday and Saturday we received a piece of meat textured like elastic which was quite difficult to eat, accompanied by leftover eggplant which was really inedible. Occasionally we received meat soup and sometimes okra fried in oil. As for the rest of the week, we usually ate rice with red lentils that was cooked with extra fried garlic resulting in heartburn, fava beans full of weevils or bean sprout cooked with garlic dressing that was again inedible. One of the prisoners described that he ate rice with his hands, then he used the bread and a piece of carton as a spoon before any actual spoons arrived!

Dinner: served before 4.00 p.m. consisted of fava beans. The food was given to us out of rusted containers or buckets, which made you feel sick just by looking at them. Despite the poor quality of the food which I couldn't eat, the grace of the Lord sustained me.

(3) Detectives (who were both colonels), were watching us including the state security investigation officer who was transferred on the 23rd September 1981, the day of my investigation.

(4) Books, daily newspapers and pens were not allowed, except for the New Testament, Agpeya (prayer book), and hymn books. Later during our incarceration, Girgis Iskandar brought us the Holy Bible including both Testaments and the Psalmody Book. [9]

Our combined program for prayers (performed together through the small openings of the cells doors) were:

• Morning Prayer at 8.00 a.m. followed by 400 prostrations (metanoia) before God in all four directions.[10]

---

9 Working at the Bishopric of Services and Secretary of the Late Bishop Samuel of Services. He was delegated from the Patriarchate to visit the priests, with the permission of the authorities.

10 Metanoia is a Greek word for prostration.

• Vespers and Twelfth Hour Prayers at 5.00 p.m., then a Bible Study led by Bishop Biemen during which we studied from the Epistles of St. Paul to the Hebrews, Philippians, Ephesians.

• Midnight Prayer at 9.00 p.m., then a prayer meeting for whoever liked to join through the cell door opening. As a compensation for not being able to pray the Holy Liturgy, we used to pray parts of it; including the litanies, commemoration, introduction of the fraction, the fraction and the Conclusion. Bishop Bishoy usually led the prayer, along with the participation of Fr. Maximus Mishriqi, Fr. Sarabamoun Abdu, Fr. Samuel Thabet and my weak self.

For two consecutive weeks we fasted on Wednesday, Thursday, and Friday.

We celebrated the vespers of El Nayrouz and the feast of the cross. These occasions were truly lovely nights. On the feast of the cross, Fr. Ibrahim Abdu made crosses out of carton boxes , which he distributed through the openings in the doors during his recess breaks. These prayers on these occasions truly displayed amazing faith.

There were stories and incidents which we heard from one of the priests every night that strengthened our faith. Amidst the pains of imprisonment, Pope Kyrillos VI and Bishop Samuel appeared in a vision to two of the reverend fathers; including Fr. Abdel Messih who was from Upper Egypt. He saw Pope Kyrillos looking sad and standing in a place without holding a stick. Pope Kryillos then said, "Finish, finish. Everything is finished" and he sat down on the couch. Fr. Tadros Yacoub from Alexandria said that he had experienced the same vision. We were greatly comforted and felt in the company of the saints. It was a wonderful night to remember the blessings of this holy patriarch and we chanted Axios for him.[11]

As for my heart and feelings in prison, they were focused on my wife, children and my daughters whom I used to mention their name with tears, asking heavenly comfort for them. All my prayers for the Lord were asking grace in His eyes, and for the victorious and struggling Church, that the Lord may bless all of us and give us comfort.[12]

I felt that the Lord answered my request when I said, "I need a retreat from the exhausting continuous work, conflicts and the conspiracies of some evil people". Humorously, the Lord wanted a 'prison retreat' with people whom I don't know closely, except for Fr. Sarabamoun Abdu, a member of one of the priests of El Giza diocese where I served.

---

11 Axios means 'Worthy' in Coptic. This hymn is chanted during Praises for the Saints.

12 The consecrated daughters at 'The Virgin Mother House for Consecrated Virgins' in Omraneyah

During the second week of imprisonment, I had such a severe stomach ache for the first time in my life and I was diagnosed with an inflammation in the left ureter. After screaming due to the severe pain, the doctor of the prison Dr. Kamal Betra came to see me. I received two injections immediately, followed by a medicine Spasmopyralgin three times a day. It was a harsh experience due to the physical pain, and my loud screams interrupted everyone. I said, "O' Lord, you know the injustice. O Virgin, don't you sympathise with me? O' Lord, why?" One of the officers gave me another blanket as we were sleeping only on a 5 cm thick mattress above the floor. On one occasion I caught a very bad flu because of the high humidity in the cell.

In another incident, one of the men who was in prison took four sleeping pills after a loud argument. When the guards were checking on the prisoners, they discovered that he was not responding. They opened his cell to check on him and thought that he had tried to commit suicide. They performed a gastric lavage using water and salt, and then issued a decree to remove all our medication. The prison guards stated that we should not use or keep anything with us which may assist in committing suicide, such as a rope, plastic thread, knife, aluminium spoon, tins, needles, and medication. This was difficult as many prisoners were prescribed medication that was critical to their health and we all called on God to intervene in this issue.

Despite these harsh living conditions, I remember the grace which the Lord granted us in the eyes of the lieutenant, officers, soldiers and detectives. They treated us nicely and apologised when the officers followed through with harsh orders or ill-treatment. Despite the fear of being reprimanded and prosecuted for not strictly following these commands, from time to time the commander kindly opened the doors of our cells while we were inside. In fact, at first the commander did this for half an hour and then for an hour. Once a detective reported the actions of this commander, orders were strictly followed until the day of our departure from El-Marg prison.

The words of the Lord are true, "If there is calamity in a city, will not the Lord have done it? Surely the Lord God does nothing, unless He reveals His secret to His servants the prophets." (Amos 3: 6-7) Also "But I am poor and needy; Make haste to me O God" (Ps 70: 5)

The name of the Coptic people who were in imprisoned at the time:

1. Bishop Bishoy of Damietta and Kafr El Sheikh. Hegumen Bishoy Lamei– Pastor of St. George Church – El Raqaqna - Gerga.

2. Dr. Adel Wahba Athanasius- a consecrate in 'Salvation of Souls'. Abdel Messih Basit Abul Kheir (High School teacher)

3. Bishop Amonious of Luxor, Esna and Armant. Bishop Bemwa

(Khory Eposkopos at El Rozayqat – Armant).

4. Dr. Nazim Fahim. Dr. Helmy El Gohary.

5. Eng. Latif Fahim Morcos. Philip Labib Iskandar – School Principal.

6. Bishop Benjamin of Menofieh. Bishop Fam of Tema and Suhad.

7. Fr. Athanasius Botros (Archangel and St. George's Church – Matareya). My weakness.

8. Dr. Nabil Rasmy Eskarous an Otolaryngology. Maher Nassif Girgis.

9. Mr. Rushdi El Sisi (Pensioner). Mr. Hikmat Farid.

10. Hegumen Zakareya Botros. Fr. Youssef Kamel (St. George's Church – Assuit).

11. Hegumen Bolos Basily. Hegume Basilious Hegumen Sidrak (Vicar of El Minya Diocese)

12. Hegumen Dawood Bolos (The Lady Virgin Church – Sadfa – Assuit. Deacon Abdel Messih Rofael (St. George's Church – Ayoub Awad village- Minya El Qamh).

13. Hegumen Girgis Rizqallah Wahba (St. George's Church – Al Max- Alexandria. Hegumen Philoppos Wefqi (St. Mary's Church – South Sahnoud - Fayyoum.

14. Mr. Adel Azer Bestawros. Dr. Fouad Fawzi Girgis.

15. Hegumen Luka Khalaf (St. George's Church – Sporting). Fr. Samuel Thabet (Cleopatra El Hammamat).

16. Hegumen Tadros Yacoub (St. George's Church – Sporting. Fr. Bishoy Yassa.

17. Fr. Ibrahim Abdo (St. George – El Geyoushi). Hegumen Abdel Messih Youssef (St. George's Church – Hager Meshta- Tahta).

18. Dr. Milad Hanna. Fr. Sarabamoun Abdo (St. Mary-Imbabah).

19. Hegumen Timothaous Milad (St. George-Suhag). Fr. Abdel Malak Riad (St. George-Suhag).

20. Mr. Ramzy Wasfi – Solicitor- (Naga Hammadi). Nazih El Qummos Botros (Ewais)

21. Dr. Shafiq Iskandar (El Kamal Pharmacy – Naga Hammadi. George Zakhary (Reserves– Alexandria)

22. Bishop Tadros of Port Said. Fr. Bishoy Fakhry (St. Bishoy Church – Port Said).

23. Bishop Wissa of Baliana. Bishop Beimen of Mallawi.

24. Mr. Fouad Youssef Abdel Malek (Deputy Minister of Ministry of Supply-Alexandria). Azmy Youssef Soliman (Ebshway Dairy Factory –Fayyoum).

25. Mr. William Faltaous (Wilson). Megally Aziz Megally (South Sanhod-Fayyoum).

26. Fr. Maximos Meshriqi (St. Mary's Church – Maragha – Suhag). Fr. Flemon Samaan (Copts' Bishopric – Tahta Shore).

27. Fr. Moussa Eissa Moussa (Suhag- El Dewayrat). Fr. Ephraim Mikhail (St. George's Church – Ezbet El Sabbagh).

28. Mr. Samir Amin Tadros. Dr. Kamal Petra (Maghagha).

DOCUMENT WRITTEN AT TIME OF INCARCERATION

Youssef Assad Qolta

Priest of The Virgin Lady – Omraneyah

Address: 14 Misr and Sudan Street, Pyramids, Giza

ID 40658 Family – El Giza Police Station

Secretariats:

L.E. Fifty- Four and Ninety -Six piasters

L.E. 54, 960

A watch brand with black arms

A necklace with a Cross

A key ring with keys

Driving License (private car)

Some personal papers and cards

Wallet + agenda + 1 key + a rubber + 3 normal pens

Signature

INVESTIGATION DAY ON WEDNESDAY 23 SEPTEMBER 1981

I was taken in for questioning on Wednesday 23rd September 1981. Usually, when a detective passes by the cell of a prisoner before being interviewed, he could prepare himself for about 5 minutes. When the detective came to me at about 7.00 a.m. I was still wearing my black garment that I hadn't taken off all during my stay at El-Marg. It only took me a few minutes to get dressed and be ready for questioning.

The lieutenant's room was full of commotion when we arrived. The lead investigator asked me for my name and then an elderly large soldier put handcuffs on my hands. I accepted these handcuffs as a gift from God, my beloved Lord Jesus Christ. For His sake, chains were placed on my hands as a criminal. Tears filled my eyes while my heart was saying, "I do not deserve this, but I'm willing to do anything for Your sake."

When I left the room, a police officer approached me saying, "Father Youssef, do you need anything?" I thanked him saying no and left. A microbus was waiting to transport us to prison. I sat in the bus between the soldier who had placed handcuffs on my hands and another soldier. Two other people also detained, Abdel Messih El Basit and Samir Amin Tadros, were also transported in the bus. I found out that the police officer driving was leading a convoy of cars. The vehicles carried the colonel, myself and the other two detainees. The cars were sounding out a siren and rotating red lamps on top of the vehicles. I felt that the bride of Christ was being led in a wedding procession around the streets, just like Jesus who carried His cross in the streets.

We travelled one hour passing through the streets of Matareya, Heliopolis, Salah Salem route, Fam El Khalig route, El Sayeda Zeinab route until we finally reached the Headquarters of the Socialist Prosecutor in Lazoghly. The leading officer drove very fast and even waved his hand and swore at other drivers if they delayed him.

The microbus stopped in front of the socialist prosecutor's door. I stepped out following the captain to a stylish elevator which took us to the 8th floor and then through a long corridor. We ended up in a waiting room where we stayed until the morning, 10.45 a.m. During this time, I was reading the Holy Bible when a soldier sitting next to me looked and advised me how to open the Bible to find God's message. I immediately followed his suggestion, though I was astonished that this Muslim man was trying to give me some biblical advice. I opened to the gospel of St. Luke chapter 22 and I felt a message from God following this man's suggestion. When I read the first verse from the Bible, the message was: "Then an angel appeared to Him from heaven, strengthening Him." (Lk 22: 23). It was a very deep, comforting experience prior to being questioned.

I waited from around 8.30 a.m. till 10.45 a.m. when they called me in for questioning. The guard took the handcuffs off my hands. I sat in front of the assistant of the socialist prosecutor on the 7th floor where they had moved me. The questioning lasted for about 20 minutes without the presence of any lawyers until my lawyers Abdel Messih Barsoum, Youssef Sharqawi, Girgis Sobhy and Louis Wissa arrived to represent me.

The questions I was asked, as far as I can remember, related to;

1- My name;

2- My age;

3- My address;

4- My job;

5- My opinion on national unity;

6- My opinion on the incidents of sectarian strife.

The accusation against me by the state security investigator was that I was the chief editor of 'The Harvest' magazine, of which an article was written inciting anti-Muslim views. At the time of the questioning, I couldn't remember the article but when I recalled it, I remembered an article titled 'A calm conversation with our brethren the non-Christians'.

After the end of the questioning the lawyers asked me, "Do you need anything?" My eyes were full of tears. I just replied, "thank you". I asked my lawyer Girgis Sobhy to remind my wife Amal about the commemoration of my father's passing during the liturgy. I farewelled my lawyers holding back tears, asking the investigator, "Don't you have the authority to open the doors of the cells because I cannot breathe from the small opening under the iron doors?" I explained to him the short duration of the recess and he replied, "let the lawyers present appeals and God will do the rest". I replied, "God is above everyone".

I came out of the investigation room and was bound in handcuffs for the third time. I thanked my lawyer Abdel Messih who told me of the congregation who were sending their greetings. I went up to the waiting room on the 8th floor, while I discovered that the investigation with Samir Amin had been postponed the following day in order that he could collect his glasses and ordinary clothes from home. Abdel Messih Basit was still under investigation. As soon as I sat down at about at 12.45 p.m., the investigator called me again to ask about the meaning of the term 'love your enemies' and what we meant by 'enemies'? He suggested that the term meant that I had participated in sectarian strife incidents. The investigation continued until about 1.15 p.m.

I returned again to the 8th floor to find that Samir and Abdel Messih were waiting for me. We left the 8th floor with the captain and caught a microbus travelling past the socialist prosecutor. As we moved from the building, I saw one of my children from church running towards me and waving. He comforted me about my son Assad and everybody else, and he also told me that Abram had joined Port Said School. The car passed by El Maleya Café and while I was waiting for the captain, I also saw one of my daughters from church running quickly towards the car and waving. At that moment I was truly comforted and felt that we could always see the Virgin and John the Beloved in the forefront of our eyes at the cross of Christ.

On our way back, the driver continued with the same reckless driving. After passing El-Marg Bridge, one of the soldier's cars had an accident, however we continued driving until we reached El-Marg Prison at around 2.30 p.m. I waited until I was placed in a cell at about 3.30 p.m. I asked myself, "is this the only defamation accusation against me from a newspaper statement and broadcast?" I prayed, "O' Lord, have mercy upon Your people, lift up the shame off Your inheritance, bring glory to Your name, church and Your servants in the entire world".

Days passed by as if they were long years, and all I could do was weep to the Lord. I experienced the meaning of the verse, "I drench my couch with my tears" (Ps 6:6). On some days I wept from morning until night. I tried in vain to sleep and wake up early. I remembered the verse, "My tears have been my food, day and night" (Ps 42: 3)

As for the 6th October 1981, it was a very strange day in El-Marg Prison. The officer came at about 8.00 a.m., opened all the cell doors and we all went out to meet him in the corridor. He informed us that H. G Bishop Samuel was visiting us straight after the military parade. The wardens had prepared Egyptian pastry, which was common food in agricultural areas, to greet him. He asked us not to raise up any issues related to the prison with him, and the wardens even cleaned and placed flowerpots at the main gate of the prison.

We all agreed that Bishop Biemen would talk on behalf of the Bishops, Hegumen Tadros Yacoub would talk on behalf of the priests and Mr. Adel Bestawros would talk on behalf of the laymen.

At 3.00 p.m. the meeting with Bishop Samuel had been postponed to another time. I became worried and couldn't sleep all night. I was cold and suffered a severe stomach ache. I tried to convert all my worrying into prayers. At 8.00 a.m. on 7th October 1981, the warden came to see us and ordered the cells to be opened but we had to remain inside them. In a very strict military tone, he said a few shocking words. "Is everyone listening to me? I'm going to talk without any questions from anyone. An emergency state has been announced in the country because of the death of the President of the Republic.... close the doors!" While he was passing by my cell, I asked eagerly, "Did he die naturally or how did he die?" He didn't respond.

A moment of silence prevailed, then voices were heard saying "Thank God" and others started expressing their joy. I said to them, "He who is glad at calamity will not go unpunished". After the warden had left, it was time for recess. I asked the police captain how President Sadat had died? He answered and said, "Be assured, Hosny Mubarak has controlled the situation. The man has died naturally at 4.00 p.m. after going back to his house". When I asked him, "Has anything happened in the country? Have the extremists done anything?" He evasively said, "Nothing". Later that evening he came back and told me the truth about Sadat being assassinated, however he didn't update us about Bishop Samuel or any of the other incidents.

I felt very anxious and asked God for protection for Egypt, the church and condolences for Sadat's family. I was telling myself that is how God interferes and judges for His children. God removed the man from earth who had bound and imprisoned the church on a day President Sadat was celebrating, which was 33 days after our imprisonment. I heard a voice saying, "The Lord prepared that the true organisers of strife would be revealed, in order that the Copts might be cleared as innocent". I said, "Glory be to God in everything. No matter the bitterness and the pain of the cross, God has seen inside the heart of this unjust judge. He was not honest with the church; thus, the Lord took his spirit according to the Bible's words: 'He shall cut off the spirit of princes'". (Ps 76: 12)

On Thursday 8th October, two days following the assassination of Sadat, I tried to find out more information about what had occurred concerning Bishop Samuel. I said to the officer, "Yesterday, I was walking with Mr. Rushdi El Sisi who is in custody with us and I said to him that I felt that Bishop Samuel has departed. What is your opinion, captain?'". I continued saying, "'I am so worried about him, I won't be upset if you tell me the truth, I just want to know so that I can pray for the Lord to manage the affairs of the church". He replied briefly, "Ok, pray". I then understood that he had departed. Around an hour after speaking with the officer, he started communicating with Bishop Biemen in front of me during recess. At about 11.00 a.m., the day after opening the cells, the officer announced the departure of Bishop Samuel. We asked him to conduct a funeral prayer for his soul the following day, on Friday at 4.00 p.m. and he agreed.

On the evening of 8th October, we prayed a brief thanksgiving prayer, the litany of the departed and the funeral exposition. We concluded our prayers with the Lord's prayer. We also had a memorial ceremony where lawyer Mr. Wilson Faltaous gave the opening speech, then my weak self, lawyer Mr. Adel Azer Bestawros, Dr. Milad Hanna, Hegumen Tadros Yacoub, and finally Anba Biemen.

On the morning of Friday 9th October, we found out from the prison guard that Bishop Samuel had been buried the previous day and that the memorial had been broadcast on television. At 4.00 p.m. the cells were opened and we lined the corridor praying the prayer of the departed on the third day of Bishop Samuel passing away. Bishop Bishoy, Fr Loqa Sidaros, Fr Samuel Thabet, Bishop Benjamin, Bishop Wissa, Bishop Biemen and myself led this prayer.

I wept during the whole funeral prayer service, but after the prayers had concluded my heart was peaceful. I prayed for Bishop Samuel, who always smiling and trying to fulfill the commandment of Christ to visit prisoners. I knew of his endurance and ability to find more than one solution to any problem. I asked God that Bishop Samuel would rest in peace in paradise. I had said in my speech, "No matter how people evaluate the role of a person at church, God, who knows the heart of each one, will reward him according to what he had offered to the Church. His loyal heart was full of love to the Church". The prison and investigation officers came to offer their condolences after we finished the prayer and returned to our cells.

During my final days in El-Marg prison, we were told about good outcomes to come. However, unfortunately we became accustomed to being misled in prison and didn't really believe anything the prison authorities said.

On Friday 16th October 1981 we were expecting to be released, however at around 2.00 p.m., the lieutenant came and said, "Everyone is to prepare his possessions and put on his attire." When the cells were opened, I asked him, "Are we being released?" He answered, "No. You're all being sent to another prison." At 4.00 p.m. we were released from our cells. It was like an imprisoned church! The clergy and laity were carrying their clothes and possessions to the lieutenant's room. We were given paper envelopes in which they had placed the items we had with us when we were imprisoned.

It was a very difficult situation for us to be escorted to another prison in a closed truck. I thought: "He permitted no one to do them wrong; Yes, He rebuked kings for their sakes" (Ps 105:14).

THE TRANSFER FROM ONE
PRISON TO ANOTHER

I placed my feet on the steps of a truck in front of me. On both sides of the truck there was a line of central security soldiers with helmets and bayonets. I found myself in a truck which may have been used to transfer dogs. I thought at least we would have been transferred in a cleaner truck and it was surprising that the truck was completely enclosed, except for four small windows about 20 cm x 10 cm in size. Also, the truck was enclosed with iron bars on both sides and we had to sit on the floor of the truck. About half of us, 28 people, were squashed into a very small area. I found a spot between Bishop Benjamin, Bishop Amonious, Bishop Tadros and Fr. Moussa. I crouched there for a while and then found a spare tyre to sit on.

The door of this truck was closed and we waited until they loaded another truck before we started moving. We didn't know where we were going or even which streets we were driving on. My heart was racing and my eyes were full of tears amidst this darkness. I could say, "For our gospel did not come to you in word only, but also in power, and in the Holy Spirit and in much assurance, as you know what kind of men we were among you for your sake." (1 Thes 1:5)

IN LIMAN WADI EL NATROUN

We exited the truck along with the central security soldiers and then entered through the narrow gate of the prison into the outer courtyard, where they asked us to line up with five people in each line. It was around 9.00 p.m. when they started a routinely writing our names in the prison record book. We then entered the inner courtyard, where we all sat on the dirty ground until the officers finished preparing the place for us. During that time my thoughts were, "is that Your gift for me, O' God? I asked for a rest and break, yet you gave me imprisonment and slander? After the tiresome struggle during the St. Mary's fast, I asked You for rest, and is that how you're responding to me?"

This persecution was such a difficult situation to accept. I do not deny that despite these feelings, the price which the church paid to have rest from persecution was a very cheap price! May God complete the rest of the struggle and grant the church peace.

The officers asked us to enter the hospital ward as it was the cleanest ward in the prison. We took our possessions into a ward measuring about 7 m x 9 m, which had three bunk beds. We were happy to be together, but it was quite noisy after such a long period of quietness in El-Marg prison.

There was a central security guard on the level above the ward. We used to hear his footsteps during the night. One night, they staged a trial which we didn't know about. A siren sounded and we heard lots of soldiers loudly calling out, which was a horrifying surprise! We thought the prison was being attacked, especially as we knew that we had been transferred because our lives were previously threatened.

We agreed upon a daily prayer program:

8.00 a.m. First & Third Hour Prayer,

12.00 p.m. Sixth- & Ninth-Hour Prayer,

5.00 p.m. Eleventh- & Twelfth-Hour Prayer,

9.00 p.m. Midnight Prayer.

The colonel specifically built a brick wall surrounding the ward in order to allow us to have our recess. This recess occurred twice a day; one hour in the morning and one hour in the evening. We were very glad because the gate of the ward was opened for us between 9.00 a.m. up till 4.00 p.m. We enjoyed the sunlight, fresh air and cold water.

After a few days, the officers granted us access to newspapers, personal clothes and outside food. This started with the arrival of food boxes from Mr. Girgis Iskander, sent by the Patriarchate, where I knew exactly where the boxes were coming from just by the way they were packaged. I was in tears for more than half an hour while my heart was crying out, "O' Lord, remember their tiresome help for me and when I'm released help me to continue to make strenuous efforts towards them." I was crying when I was eating the cake, knowing who made the cake just by the way it was cut and placed in the box.

Dr. Milad Hanna was one of the first prisoners to be investigated. He was truly a humble scholar who respected the opinion of his opponents. He slept in the bunk bed right above me. On the first day of his investigation, he brought us a bag of guava fruit and some biscuits. He also brought biscuits on the following day, but the authorities decided to move him to Turah prison. Farewelling him was quite touching and he addressed us with a speech that was followed by Bishop Biemen. Dr. Hanna shook hands with each one of us individually, and while he was farewelling me, he looked at everybody and said, "I recommend that you give Fr. Youssef five minutes to lead in prayers each day so that you may be comforted like me." Shortly after Dr. Hanna left, he sent a message about an article which his wife Evelyn Riad had written in "Akher Saa" magazine entitled "A Snapshot". I wept and prayed for this honest woman when I read her article.

Despite the challenges of being imprisoned in El-Marg it was a wonderful period of spiritual struggle! I used to wake up at 3.00 a.m. to pray and make prostrations until 6.00 a.m. Then I would read the bible and finish the books such as Ezekiel, Daniel, Joshua until first Kings, and all the books of the minor prophets. We then began our communal daily routine ending in prayers often accompanied with tears. I would usually sleep early around 7.00 p.m. despite the noise surrounding me and would encourage others also to sleep early.

I spent most of my recess time wondering around alone in sincere prayer, except for a few times when I spoke with other prisoners. I was trying to avoid talking too much, which could be quite distracting. I likened this chatter to a ball being kicked by different people. I tried to apply this verse from Amos the Prophet, "Therefore the prudent keep silent at that time, for it is an evil time." (Amos 5: 13). I tried to apply this practice as wisely as possible.

I received numerous letters of support and gifts which moved me. One in particular, a hand-written note that I received from my wife Amal on 10th November 1981 celebrating our wedding anniversary was quite moving. My tears would not cease and my heart was beating fast. I also received another handwritten message from her on top of a black forest cake and a handwritten message from my beloved children Abram and Asaad. I wept a lot when I read Abram's letter which contained a statement, "I go to school riding the bus now. What do you think dad?" How could I tell him what I thought? Asaad wrote to me, "Eat well and sleep early so that you come back to us as beautiful as the moon". The officer did not allow me to keep these messages. Everyone enjoyed eating from the cake, except that I was so emotional and anxious that I couldn't eat from it. "O' Lord do not allow these days to be repeated and forgive, O' Lord, those who had allowed it to happen!"

I also received a handwritten letter from one of the consecrated sisters reassuring me about their wellbeing and asking advice about fasting. She informed me that all the sisters had participated in preparing the food that I received. I returned a message stating that I was concerned about them.

On 10th November 1981 we held a celebration for the ordination anniversary of Fr. Athanasius Botros and my wedding anniversary. Anba Bishoy talked about the service of the priest and his wife, and then chanted worthy (Axios)! I felt deep bitterness when going to bed and called on the Lord.

On 15th November 1981, the investigations continued for some of the other prisoners. These prisoners were transported in a truck to the socialist prosecutor for at least a four-hour trip each way. On the third day of the investigation of Anba Beimen the truck broke down twice and returned back to the prison at 2.30 a.m.

At about 1 p.m. on Friday 20th November 1981, we were called and transported in trucks. The only difference this time was that we knew we were going to El-Marg prison. We were instructed that we each had to carry our own mattresses and blankets that the 26 of us had used onto the truck by any means. We started moving at about 2.30 p.m. I crouched down between Anba Amonious, Anba Fam, Anba Bemwa, Anba Biemen, Anba Benjamin, Anba Bishoy and Fr. Athanasius Botros. Anba Bishoy made 'Halawa' sandwiches and distributed them with flasks of tea. I did not eat until the end of the journey when we found ourselves in front of El-Marg prison's gate at 5.45 p.m., where we started our next stage of imprisonment.

IN EL-MARG PRISON ONCE AGAIN

On the evening of Friday 20th November 1981, we returned to El-Marg Prison. We had our pens with us and I started writing a draft of this account from Monday 23rd November 1981 at 3.35 p.m. in a small notepad. I then copied my draft in a notebook which I bought on Saturday 5th December 1981 from the canteen for 15 Piasters.

The officers took us to ward 6, which was a hall around 6 m x 20 m. There were five windows on both sides with iron bars, an iron door, and a bathroom which had four old-fashioned toilets and three basins for washing. Most of the windows were without glass. That night we slept on mattresses on the floor, covered with two blankets from the prison and another blanket which the patriarchate had sent to us from Wadi El Natroun.

I had another episode of dizziness and blurred vision causing two falls at 3.00 a.m. and 8.00 a.m. on 22nd November 1981. After Dr. Nabil Rasmy Eskarous examined me, he said that it was an inflammation of the eustachian tube in the middle ear that caused an imbalance in my body. Thus, I thanked God that it was not high blood pressure or poor blood circulation. Dr. Eskarous gave me nose drops to use three times daily and one tablet nightly for allergies. Thank God I was recovering well from the inflammation, and the next day the doctor advised me to continue with the medications. Thank You, O' Lord, for You said: "I am the Lord your Healer."

On the eve of 23rd November 1981, we prayed vespers for St. Mina's feast. On Tuesday 24th November 1981, the guards began installing three bunk beds in each cell, like the ones we had in

Wadi El-Natroun. After much chaos in installing the three bunk beds, the prisoners who were with me were Dr. Nabil Attallah Soliman (a surgeon from Suhag), Dr. Farid Shafiq Sawiros, (a surgeon at Naga Hammadi Hospital) and Dr Wasfi Riad Morcos. Bishop Bishoy and Deacon Mesiha Rafael willingly slept on the floor at their own request. The guards allowed us food from outside, and newspapers and letters after they had been initially screened. Later, the guards relaxed further in their security and the letters came directly to Girgis who then distributed them accordingly to the correct recipients. On the opposite ward 5, we found our brethren who were in Abu Zaabal prison transferred to Wadi El Natroun and they left one day before us.

I received a letter with some toffee from my wife Amal and the children, which I gave to Bishop Bishoy to distribute among us. I also received tissue packs and some peanuts. My heart was troubled and I felt that something harmful may have happened to my family. I prayed to the Lord to safely protect them all. "Up until now, O' Lord, I am asking for Your comfort."

The investigations were conducted quickly among us. The following day the officers took 25 prisoners and each one came back recounting the trifle issues which they were accused of. My pain and crying increased, and I asked God for forgiveness for the person who was the cause of this bitterness that I was suffering from.

On the morning of 24th November 1981, I received a bouquet of flowers and perfume, a comb in a bag with some imported apples and bananas from my son, and a cake with two boxes of vegetarian sweets that was probably given by the consecrated deaconesses. Bishop Bishoy distributed everything among us. I received the gifts trying to hold back tears while everyone was congratulating me in the ward. Truly I was thanking God for His favour towards me and the church. Help me O' Lord to always be a living sacrifice, a servant, giving everything to Your sons and daughters to find comfort and joy in You. That day, I remembered all those who accepted to carry the cross with me for 14 years of priesthood, particularly my wife, my fathers the priests, and all my faithful children.

Remember O' Lord the salvation of my soul and eternal life. Protect Your love in my heart, the love of Your church and service of its children. Remember O' Lord all those whom I have served faithfully and who given me a hard time. All those who resisted and angered me, forgive them and myself. Make these days a reason to work inside their hearts and grant me grace in their eyes to keep serving everyone, despite their negative attitude towards me. May every year pass by without You regretting that You have chosen me. I pray that You grant my weakness a new chance for repentance and growth in love and purity.

On 25th November 1981, we received a message from Bishop Arsanious of El Menya asking about me. I also met one of my children from church and he reassured me about the progress of our church. He informed me that they had started and nearly finished painting the bookshop. I asked about Fr. Rafael and he informed me that he had surgery on his toe and Fr Kyrollos and Fr. Luke were helping him pray liturgies on Friday and Sunday.

Thank You O' Lord, for this joyful news. Make my heart rejoice in Your work at church, especially while I'm absent. Let Your blessing dwell among all the servants, children and congregation from generation to generation. Let Your living presence on the altar of this church attract souls and unite hearts during my absence.

At 3.30 a.m., a soldier came calling Mr. Samir Amin Tadros to transfer him to another prison after he had requested to join the imprisoned politicians in Turah. The officers did not confirm where he was being transferred, but we assumed Turah prison. Mr. Tadros left the ward at 5.10 a.m. We all woke up early before his departure, reflecting on the 12 weeks spent together. He was a kind and honest man, accepting humiliation for the sake of his extreme opinions. We never really agreed with him, and because of his extreme ideas he had many disagreements with Bishop Bishoy who didn't approve of his opinions most of the time.

Remember O' Lord his repentance and eternal life. Let these days plant in him a desire for eternal life. Remember his service among us and his wife for whom I pleaded with You for her sake as soon as I met him in Turah prison.

On the same day at 1.00 p.m., Fr. Samuel Thabet was taken to Al Manyal University Hospital to treat a kidney stone in his left ureter. We later received a letter from him with Anba Bishoy, which he sent with a Muslim person who was under investigation, in which he assured us that he had a separate room and the conditions were better than the wards. He also told us that only one room separated him from Omar El Telmesany, who knocked on his door asking about him as soon as he had arrived, and they had long conversations together.[13] This happened on the day of Anba Bishoy's investigation.

On 28th November 1981 at around 12 p.m. I was reading the Holy Bible and was informed that some visitors were waiting for me in the officer's room. In fact, Amal, Cecile, Mimi, Phoebe, and others came to visit. Tears were about to flow from my eyes and I stuttered speaking. Amal had lost a lot of weight. She was wearing a new dark blue dress with a white collar. A visitation for a prisoner is very important psychologically, as it allows one to feel that there is someone that actually cares about him. Visits can also be important physically, notably one can bring some

13 Omar El Telmesany was a terrorist from the Muslim brotherhood who had been imprisoned by Sadat.

nutritious food to compensate for the normally bland meals.

Thank You, O' Lord, for granted me the feelings of the prisoner whose relatives visit and bring him food. Reward them for everything they have brought to me.

Amal informed me on the visit that the officers did not search the house and that many people came to visit and try to comfort her. She told me that a tremendous amount of people was waiting for me to return home. Amal also told me that she had permission to visit me with the children the following Friday and that the solicitors told her that there was nothing incriminating on my file. They told her that the decision for my release had been issued, but an actual date suspended. O' Lord let it be according to Your will. Amal also told me that Bishop Domadius was weeping all the time. May the Lord, remember and sustain him.

I thank You O' Lord in every condition, no matter about my feelings and many tears. Please control everything between Your hands. O' Lord, the bitter which You choose for me is better than the honey which I choose for myself!

At night, I was invited to address a sermon in our neighbouring ward 5, accompany Fr. Maximous Mishriqi to lead the eleventh- and twelfth-hour prayers, and lead the hymn lesson which lasted from 7.00 p.m. till 9.00 p.m. During the visit, Dr. Nuzhi Zaki gave me a notebook and pen to write a story about the good works in the life of Fr. Mikhail Ibrahim, whom I had previously spoken about with him. I was astonished to find a notebook and pen. He also gave me another notebook for my personal use. I was overjoyed in the Lord who out of His generosity gave me paper at 2 a.m. and provided me with a whole notebook in the evening!!

On the 4th December 1981, notebooks and pens arrived at the canteen. I was grateful to have more notebooks, and initially decided to wait until I was released to rewrite what I had written in tiny letters in prison, but through these notebooks God provided a means to write my feelings and points in detail. Thank You O' Lord, please sustain me to finish....

THE FEELINGS OF A PRISONER

The general rule of life in prison is 'protect yourself'. The soldier protects himself from the officer, while the officer protects himself from the investigator and so on. Lying is common practice in prison, along with the system of bribery such as exchanging cigarettes among prisoners for prison services (laundry, barber, cleaning, etc.). Everything has a price! The forbidden things are permitted through contraband exchange!

Conversations among everyday prisoners are commonly about being released from prison, such as the feast of the prophet Muhammad.[14] Other prisoners speak about the news which they have heard from some of the visitors, daily newspapers or received in letters. They rely on these things to lift their spirits. Many scholars and lawyers that were imprisoned wept and were physically unwell. For the true Christian prisoners, however, they have different conversations. Their best attitude is captured in the biblical words, "Therefore the prudent keep silent at that time, for it is an evil time" (Amos 5: 13). I was astonished that so many prisoners focused on the temporary issues or daily problems. The wise and prudent person is a rare coin.

On Sunday 6th December 1981 at around 10.00 a.m. I received a message that there was a visitation for me. This was just my second time to receive a visitor and my emotions were calmer. I was truly glad to see my sons, Abram and Asaad.

Thank You O' Lord for their good health, and I ask You to reward Amal and whoever participated with her in looking after them. I need to offer many thanksgivings sacrifices to pour under Your feet.

Mimi, Fifi and Aida also came to visit along with my family. Mimi

---

14 Omar El Telmesany was a terrorist from the Muslim brotherhood who had been imprisoned by Sadat.

told me that Cecile had passed me her greetings. The visit was at the office of the investigator and next to him was Bishop Beimen and Dr. Nabil from Suhag. Amal informed me that the blessings of the Lord were plenty, and that the food which we received in boxes yesterday was sent from them. This was the third delivery of food we had received. Amal also informed me that sister Samiha and all the nuns were praying for me, while the lawyers did not charge any money for their work.[15] O' Lord compensate their work, reward them and grant success for Your work through them.

Abram told me that he needed prayers for his upcoming French and Science exams. It was the first time for me to know that he was studying French at the new school. Help him O' Lord and grant him success. He brought me a lolly bag and a 1982-year calendar, while Fr. Youssef Hanna sent me his regards. Remember O' Lord his feelings and concern. As for Asaad, he had put on a bit of weight after his last illness. He asked me to pray for him and told me that he was grossly reading the Bible. O' Lord, grant success to both of my children and spiritual children which You have given to me. Let them also be my children in the Spirit, having a share in Your kingdom with myself and Amal. Grant them understanding, which You granted to Daniel the Prophet, and the success which You had granted to Joseph the Righteous. Pour Your Spirit upon their faces and grant them

---

15 The Manager and nuns of St. Joseph School at Zamalek

grace in the eyes of their teachers.

Someone told me that the investigation officer had a meeting with the consecrated deaconesses in the presence of the Metropolitan and had taken information about them. He kept trying, in vain, to gain incriminated information about me. O' Lord forgive the officer and me, because I said to her while I was in a bad temper, 'May God punish him'. Amal was more righteous than me and said to me that they were preparing a present to give the officer when I was released. O' Lord help us to obey Your commandments which You have taught Your children to help me in my weakness. Yes, O' Lord, help me to pray for his sake and be good to him, following Your commandment, which You had promised and said, "Most assuredly, I say to you, if anyone keeps My word, he shall never see death." (Jn 8:51) But if I say, "since it is a righteous thing with God to repay with tribulation those who trouble you…" (1 Thes. 1: 6). O' Lord, deal with him according to Your will.

I had mixed emotions by this stage. I was ready to remain in prison if this was the price for preventing information about Your daughters reaching the investigation department. O' Lord, You know what could happen, but if this had happened while I was in prison, during hard circumstances and at the presence of the father Bishop who is primarily responsible before You, clear me O' Lord from this responsibility forever. Although I was repeating with Saint Paul, "I now rejoice in my sufferings for you, and fill up in my flesh what is lacking in the afflictions of Christ, for the sake of His body, which is the church." (Col 1: 24).

I was really sad to know that they had taken information about the deaconesses that could potentially lead to their imprisonment. I never heard of this in any consecration house or convent. I don't know if You O' Lord want to let Your beloved daughters enter this cross. Let it be according to Your will for the glory of Your name, but I cry out to You to protect their souls and bodies from the threat of prison! Yes, O' Lord, do not let me witness the day when I see my son or my daughter imprisoned as my emotions will be raging. You know that I cannot tolerate to see this. Through the intercession of the Virgin Mary, and Your Blood which was shed for us, let the growth of their life be in Your fear, peace, calmness and joy. Glory be to You in everything, O Almighty God.

Someone had sewed a tunic for me which Amal brought with her. May the Lord, reward and protect her soul and body. I asked Amal about my friends and she assured me that they were all well. She brought Holy bread from St. Mina's Monastery in Mariout and holy oil, which felt like St. Mina and Pope Kyrillos visited me in prison themselves.

That evening, we prayed Vespers in commemoration of Bishop

and Martyr Anba Sarabamoun, led by Bishop Benyamin. Fr. Sarabamoun Abdu addressed us about the life of the saint and was followed by a speech from Bishop Benyamin about repentance.

7 DECEMBER 1981

I thank God it's 2.30 p.m. and I haven't eaten anything up until now. I've written the final copy of the diary entries on a small notepad written on Saturday 21st November 1981, when they allowed us to have access to paper and a pen. There were many visitations on this day. We knew that Anba Beimen's brother asked yesterday to visit within the next 15 days but was refused due to our release from prison being scheduled within that time.

Several items were brought from the doctor's union to help improve the conditions in prison; including a sponge mattress, a blanket, a change of clothes, face towel and a bed. I heard, after the doctor's meeting with the delegate of the doctor's federation, that the delegate had met the President in the parliamentary residence and said that we would be released sooner than anyone could imagine! This all depended on the decision of the President. But I see that it all depends on Your good perfect pleasant will, O Almighty, let it be according to Your will, glory be to You in everything.

At night, we held a seminar about the topic of confession led by Anba Bishoy, which started with some questions from Mr. Adel Azer among many other participants.

8 DECEMBER 1981

I was awake early by 3.45 a.m. when I met Mr. Rushdi El Sisi in front of the wash basins and he said to me in English, "Two days. Don't tell anyone". He was so happy, then I saw him writing this in a notebook. As for me, O' Lord, I don't bother about any dates but I'm calling You from the depth of my heart, as You have taught me. Let it be according to Your will, as You have trained me to let go of everything easily. As long as You are preparing everything for me, I am so ashamed to ask for anything else.

Today they took Anba Fam, Hegumen Timothaous Milad and Dr. Wasfy Riad from ward 6 for investigation. They also took seven others from ward 5. They came back from the investigations by 3.30 p.m. and they said that a group would be released by Wednesday or Thursday.

I started today to re-write some thoughts and meditations about the second time period of imprisonment in El-Marg. A strong feeling came to me to prepare my bag, and God willing, while the ward is quiet, I will try to do it today.

On this day, the Lord gave me grace in the eyes of two young prisoners whom I used to give them food. One of the prisoners gave me a bucket of hot water to bathe for the first time in about four months. I haven't even bathed at all since I came to this prison. Also, other prisoner washed my clothes. Help me O' Lord, to visit these two prisoners after I'm released. Use me, more and more for the glory of Your name.

I received a letter today which was sent to a brother in custody with us. Remember him and all his children. Reward him O' Lord for checking up on me, according to Your command, "I was in prison and you came to Me." (Mt 25:36)

The way that the food was set out in the box which arrived today gives me the impression that it was from Omraneyah. At night, a seminar was held in which Mr. Adel Azer Bestawros addressed us about the 'Act of Punishments', succeeded by Mr. Rushdi El Sisi. It was like a farewell party that felt we would all be released soon. He concluded with a speech 'Between El-Marg and Wadi El Natroun.'

I read an article in 'Al Ahram' written by Dr. Nawal Sadawi titled 'It happened on the morning of 25th November 1981', which resonated many of my feelings and emotions as a prisoner.

Additionally, today is the 40th day commemoration of Mr.

Abdul Messih Hanna's wife. May the Lord repose her soul and grant comfort to her husband and children. Please convey my feelings to them and remind Amal to do what is appropriate towards them.

9 DECEMBER 1981

Today, eight members from ward 6 and another ten members from ward 5 were called into investigation. At 4.00 a.m. I had a strong feeling that I was about to leave and should start packing my things, but I delayed packing up. I received a letter from Fr. Mina Ibrahim, priest of St. Mina's Church at Shobra, sending me his greetings when he came outside the ward of the doctors' clinic. May the Lord reward him.

I started having flu symptoms today and laid in bed all day. Today, Anba Biemen spoke about the introduction of St. John's Gospel.

Today my feelings and thoughts were followed by these questions:

1- Will I still be serving at El Omraneyah or will I be sent somewhere else? Would this fulfil the condition of praying at the same church and altar upon which I was ordained?

2- Should I immigrate with my family to try and avoid this saga ever happening again? Should I discuss the matter with my immediate family only, or also with my sisters and their husbands?

3- What would the situation be for the consecrated deaconesses whom I bear a responsibility before God? Would this decision hinder the idea of consecration and deter others?

4- Would my decisions affect the spiritual and psychological development of my two sons, Abram and Asaad?

5- What should I do now towards those who have defamed me? What has been their attitude towards me during my absence? How would this affect my spirituality and personal behaviour in service and life?

6- What is the best way to deal with the officer whose false report was the initial reason for being placed in custody? Should I give him a present? Should I even meet him again, and if so, how and where?

7- How should I serve the stubborn male servants and exhausted female servants? What has happened in the service during my absence? Have the servants performed their duties or have they fled away, been slack or afraid?

8- How has my absence affected my service towards non-Christians and the Christian congregation?

9- What is the current situation of the youth meeting, servants meeting and the other services, especially the service of the poor?

10- What are the urgent needs of the consecrated deaconesses?

11- What should be the best system for confession? How should I meet the congregation if I'm still serving El Omraneyah? How exactly should I do visitations and how often?

12- How do I express my good feelings towards my lawyers and to all those who exhausted great efforts for my sake when I was in custody?

13- What is the best way of keeping in touch with those whom I have spent time in prison, especially on special occasions and commemorations of their ordination? How should I organise visiting the prisoners who served me while in custody and try to meet their needs?

These thoughts kept me busy throughout the day. I am placing them between Your hands, O' Lord and let it be according to Your will. I remembered that with just one paper I made a small notebook that led to a final written book.

These experiences and plenty more gave me the perspective
that there really is no problem without a solution in God's eyes.
One must work wisely to become a tool which God uses to utter
lifegiving words to the souls who are suffering.

10 DECEMBER 1981

Today four prisoners from our ward and 16 prisoners from ward
5 were called for questioning. Someone came and asked for
the names of those who were over 60 years old. I asked why
and they just said that the head of the prisoner's organisation
had asked for it. Let it be according to Your will, O' Lord, let
them release the elderly prisoners. At the same time a message
came from Bishop Paula to Bishop Bishoy saying that visits were
being made to H.H Pope Shenouda III.

Fr. Sarabamoun Abdo brought koshary today in pots from
St. Mary's church in Imbabah.[16] His wife had met H.G. Bishop
Domadius, who wept whenever he saw her as many servants
in his diocese had been imprisoned. Bishop Damadius told her
that the investigation officer visited him a short while ago and
informed him that we would all be released soon. Let it be
according to Your will, O' Lord.

---

16 Koshary is a meal generally combined of rice, lentils and pasta.

Mr. Philip told me about the non-Christian school deputy who made a false complaint against him and was the reason he had been taken into custody. An undercover investigation officer told him that they were in El Zawya country investigating Mr. Philip. The school deputy told him, "It's true that we complained about him unjustly", then he was asked, "So he didn't do anything wrong?" He answered, "Not at all". The officer then took the school deputy into prison for investigation! That's how You are just, O' Lord, as You have done, do it for the glory of Your Name.

Today is my son Abram's birthday. Let it also be according to Your will, O' Lord, as I wasn't present on this occasion. Accept my prayers for Abram's sake, to become a son of blessing, inheriting a blessing from Your pure mouth and to be successful before You. May he be a blessing to our family. Protect him, O' Father, who cares for sensitive souls. He is Your son. Grant him understanding in French and Science according to his request. Show him Your glory, grant him grace in the eyes of his teachers, and grant him to complete the housework with his mother. Restore to me the opportunity to celebrate this occasion together yearly as an entire household until the end of our lives. Through the intercession of the Virgin Mary, Amen.

A strange coincidence is that Arsani, Fr. Luka Sidaros son's birthday is also today. The clergy and laity sang happy birthday to Arsani and Abram. Thank You, O' Lord. During the prayers, Anba Bishoy prayed for them as well as most of the other fathers. O' Lord accept their prayers.

11 DECEMBER 1981

Today Saad Tawfiq and his wife Amal, accompanied by Mr. Asaad Rizq, came to visit Dr. Kamal Betra. They asked Dr. Kamal to pass on their greetings and told him that my son Abram was fine. O' Lord reward them for caring for me and bless them. In the evening, Dr. Magdy gave me a letter from Asaad Rizq who made us tea and we sat together in joy for more than half an hour. O' Lord, reward Asaad for his letter and for asking about me.

I slept late, due to many prayers and tears.

12 DECEMBER 1981

This day marks the feast of the entry of the Virgin Mary to the temple and 103 days spent in prison. Today also, Anba Amonious was taken from our ward for investigation, while another six people from ward 5 were taken for questioning.

After drinking tea Dr. Kamal Betra called and told me that Anba Wissa wanted to see. When I saw him, Anba Wissa told me about a dream he had yesterday. He dreamt that he saw a plane blow up and someone screaming 'Nabawy Ismail is inside it'. He then saw me (Fr Youssef Assad) with a bright, shining face. Several white doves flew to our prison ward, and many people were kissing and congratulating us! Fr. Philopos Wifqi interpreted the plane in the dream as thoughts. The explosion on the plane means that the thought of this person has blown up. As for the doves, they are the thoughts of God which are fulfilled. His vision of myself as the prisoner was that all the prisoners in the ward were joyful and illuminating as there were being released.

Today, I read a nice article for 'Mustafa Amin' in Akhbar Al Yum Newspaper about our status. Let Your voice O' Lord be uttered. This article and the one of Ibrahim Nafe yesterday in 'Al Ahram' could be a precursor to the people for our release. At the same time, apparently 'Akhbar Al Yum' published a proclamation of terrorism to prepare people for our release. I have yielded my life to You, O' Lord to do whatever You like. At each moment, let me be consecrated, in all my senses, to You O' my Beloved. You have looked after me and I am unworthy.

It was a surprise for me today to be requested outside to visit one of my spiritual daughters. I sat with her for around about half an hour and she felt comforted. However, she did complain about a speech given by Sadat to report any girl who was kidnapped or heard disobeying her parents. A man who was the father of a consecrated deaconess had sent a complaint for investigation. After due process in the presence of eight consecrated deaconesses and a Metropolitan, the outcome was a negative report into the incident. The father of this deaconess then wept and said to the Bishop "forgive me." Someone said to me, "when you are released, you will find that God has changed a lot of people."

My spiritual daughter reassured me about our church after I asked if there was any opposition towards the state of the church – including publishing books and cassette tapes. She told me that someone tried to obstruct justice in the criminal cases after I was arrested, but through the grace of God she was able to oppose any opposition to our church and its members. She also mentioned the positive progress of the consecrated deaconesses. I rejoiced in their work for God, and the grace which He gave to them in the eyes of bishop Anba Paula and Anba Biemen. Just seeing them praise God couldn't equal all the days of my imprisonment! My spiritual daughter told me that Fr. Morcos Daoud is her confession father now and that there are 90 nursing babes in childcare. Additionally, this spiritual daughter informed me that Fr. Salib Sorial was very kind with them and visited Amal at home. It was the first time since I had been imprisoned that I had sat with someone for that long. I felt a feeling of freedom as there was only one officer and detective to supervise us together! Maybe it was a present from St. Mary on the feast of her entry into the temple.

At 1.30 p.m. sharp, the detective stopped us and instructed me to write the following:

"The Honourable General Socialist Prosecutor in Cairo,

Greetings,

Presented to your honour from Fr. Youssef Asaad Qolta, priest of St. Mary's Church, Omraneyah.

I pledge that I will not carry out any political or religious activity against the current rule.

This is an acknowledgment for me for the above mentioned

Fr. Youssef Asaad Qolta"

12/12/1981

We all rejoiced greatly in the ward and kissed each other as this meant that our imprisonment was coming to an end.

Hegumen Zakareya Botrous wrote some thoughts about our imprisonment which he titled 'the disadvantages and difficulties of the cell':

1- The name of these cells was called 'the Trial'. When I asked about the reason for the name, I was told that this ward was specialised for the worst prisoners. Thus, the name of the ward describes 'calamity' or 'bitter trial'.

2- There was pitch darkness in the cell by 4.00 p.m. In summer the lights were turned on from 4.30 p.m. till 10.00 p.m. "Truly the light is sweet, and it is pleasant for the eyes to behold the sun" (Ecc 11: 7).

3- The tight cells gave us the impression that we were in a tomb, potentially leading us to severe psychological depression. The height of the cell was only 180 cm.

4- The prison cells had poor ventilation that was almost unbearable in summer.

5- The atmospheric pressure inside the cell would make you feel dizzy when standing for three minutes, thus one had to lean on the wall or door.

6- Being banned from any news and completely cut off the outside world was as if we were in the valley of the shadow of death.

7- A world of full of lies; if we would ask anyone a question, we usually receive a quick answer but later discover that it was a lie. Communication between us was done through the tiny opening in the door (10 cm x 10 cm) asking, "What's the latest lie?" These questions were whispered as we returned from recess.

8- Being forbidden from communication with each other was difficult; recess was taken in turns with each cell to limit communication between inmates, though later multiple cells simultaneously took recess at any given time.

9- The cells were filled with groups of large mosquitoes, nearly the size of a fly, because of the presence of a lake sewerage next to the outer fence of the prison.

10- The walls of the cell were often stained with the blood of mosquitoes due to our repeated attempts to kill them, usually with shoes and slippers.

11- A layer of thick black mould covering the toilet walls could easily make you feel sick.

12- The same basin tap was used for the following:

a. Washing your face and hands

b. Drinking water

c. Washing the dishes

d. Washing food

13- Being imprisoned with one person had its difficulties, some of which included:

a. Different customs and habits between each person

b. Sharing the same toilet without a curtain or door

c. The area space for sleeping was only about 80 cm.

14- The eating utensils were also used for cleaning tiles, which could easily make you feel sick.

15- The buckets of food were exposed to the flies and often cockroaches could be seen in the food. The bread was also exposed to flies.

16- The prisoners responsible for cleaning the bathrooms and sweeping and mopping the cells, were almost always the same people to distribute food and bread.

17- Paper, pens and newspapers were forbidden, except the Holy Bible and (Agpeya) prayer book.

18- Sudden random inspection of our cells could recurringly happen at any time.

19- If anyone disobeyed instructions the entire ward members would be punished. This would result in less time spent during recess, making it more difficult for a prisoner to complete his daily tasks.

20- The day would end at 2.00 p.m. at the trial ward. Both the cell door and outer ward door were locked with keys. The prison guard would then hand the key to the administration office while he stayed outside the ward, together with two officers from the state security and prison investigation.

21- We struggled psychologically, despite much prayer and meditation. Our condition gradually deteriorated and several times one of us collapsed due to the mental pressure of living in such a harsh place. In fact, the pressure was so great to the extent that one of the laymen tried to commit suicide by consuming excessive amounts of anti-depressant pills. All sharp tools, belts and leather crosses were confiscated from the prisoners to reduce the potential risk of one committing suicide.

22- Bathing; there was only one bath in a cell with two showers that were separated by a small wall without a door or curtain. Bathing time did not exceed 10 minutes and the prison guard would open the bathroom door and resort to physically pulling the naked prisoner outside if his time was up.

On the 11 p.m. news we heard the release of 17 of the politicians who were prosecuted by the state security prosecution. These politicians were also charged with co-operating with a foreign country through a group of journalists and solicitors. Their release was announced at 8.00 p.m. on the BBC, while we are looking forward to our turn, O' Lord!

13 DECEMBER 1981

We heard on the BBC that the Pope would return to the Patriarchate to resume his clerical duties and pray the Christmas liturgy at St. Mark's Cathedral.

We heard 'the Voice of Arabs' broadcast that the socialist prosecutor had issued a decree to release 17 other prisoners as well as 16 journalists.

At all times, let it be only according to Your will O' Lord, You who are the Pantocrator.

Document written at time of incarceration

Youssef Assad Qolta

Priest of The Virgin Lady Church – Omraneyah

Address: 14 Misr and Sudan Street, Pyramids, Giza

ID 40658 Family – El Giza Police Station

Secretariats:

L.E. Fifty- Four and Ninety -Six piasters

L.E. 54, 960

A watch brand with black arms

A necklace with a Cross

A key ring with keys

Driving License (private car)

Some personal papers and cards

Wallet + agenda + 1 key + a rubber + 3 normal pens

Signature

…… …… …… .

APPENDIX

POPE SHENOUDA III

THE 16 BOOKS COMPOSED BY POPE SHENOUDA
WERE THE FOLLOWING:

1. God is all I need.

2. Presence with God.

3. May the Lord answer you.

4. Contemplations on Maundy Thursday.

5. Contemplations on Good Friday.

6. Spiritual watchfulness.

7. Spiritual vigilance.

8. Returning to God.

9. Many years of people's questions (Part 1).

10. Many years of people's questions (Part 2).

11. How do we start a new year?

12. Inspiration from the Nativity.

13. Spirituality of fasting.

14. Life of repentance and purity.

15. Life of faith.

16. Diabolical wars.

BISHOPS WHO WERE IMPRISONED WITH
HH POPE SHENOUDA III

1. Bishop Bishoy of Domyat in cell 1.

2. Bishop Wisa of El-Balina in cell 23.

3. Bishop Beimen of Malawy in cell 23.

4. Bishop Amonious of Luxur in cell 3.

5. Bishop Benyamin of El-Monofeya in cell 6.

6. Bishop Tadros of Port Said in cell 22.

7. Bishop Fam of Tamma in cell 6.

8. Bishop Bemwa, abbot of the monastery of St George in El-Rezkiat in Luxur in cell 3.

LIST OF THE TWENTY-FOUR PRIESTS WHO WERE IMPRISONED WITH HIS HOLINESS:

1. Fr Boules Basili. Cell 11 – St Mary Church – El-wogooh St – Shobra, Cairo. He was a member of the People's Assembly in Shobra, and president of the Karma Committee.

2. Fr Zacharia Botros. Cell 10 – St Mark Church – Cleopatra St – Masr El-Gedida, Cairo.

3. Fr Abdel-Maseeh Rizk. Cell 12 – St George Church – Sporting, Alexandria.

4. Fr Tadros Yacoub Malaty. Cell 17 – St George Church – Sporting, Alexandria.

5. Fr Louka Khalaf Sidarous. Cell 15 - St George Church – Sporting, Alexandria.

6. Fr Philobos Wafky. Cell 12 – St Mary Church – Village of Sanhour in the west, El-Fayyoum.

7. Fr Dawood Boules. Cell 13 – St Bishay and St Peter Church – District of Sadfa, Asiut.

8. Fr Abdel-Maseeh Yousif. Cell 29 –St George Church – Hagar Mashta – Tahta, Souhag.

9. Fr Samuel Thabet Azzer. Cell 15 – St Mary Church – Cleopatra, Alexandria.

10. Fr Bishoy Fakhry. Cell 22 – St Bishoy Church – Port Said.

11. Fr Ephraim Fr Mikhail. Cell 26 – The Church of Ezbet El-Sabbagh – Tammah, Souhag.

12. Fr Basilius Sidrak Isaac. Cell 11 – St Mark Church – Diocese of El-Menia.

13. Fr Yousif Kamel. Cell 10 – St George Church – Asiut.

14. Fr Maximous Meshreky. Cell 27 – St Mary Church – El-Maragha, Asiut.

15. Fr Philemon Fr Samaan. Cell 27 – St George Church – Hagar Mashta – Tahta, Souhag.

16. Fr Timothy Milad. Cell 19 – St George Church – Souhag.

17. Fr Abdel-Malak Riad. Cell 19 – St George Church – Souhag.

18. Fr Mousa Issa Mousa. Cell 26 – St Mina Church – El-Dowayrat, Souhag.

19. Fr Bishoy Lamey. Cell 1 – St George Church – El-Rakakna, Gerga.

20. Fr Yousif Assad. Cell 7 – St Mary Church – El-Omranya, Giza.

21. Fr Athanasius Boutros Soliman. Cell 7 – Church of Archangel Michael and St George – Ezbet El-Rayes – Matarya, Cairo.

22. Fr Sarabamoun Abdo. Cell 29 – St Mary Church – Embabah, Giza.

23. Fr Ibrahim Abdo. Cell 16 – St George Church – El-Gioshy St –

Shobra, Cairo.

24. Fr Bishoy Yassa Zaki. Cell 17 – St George Church – Masr El-Gedida, Cairo.

www.ingramcontent.com/pod-product-compliance
Lightning Source LLC
LaVergne TN
LVHW091253080426
835510LV00007B/243